I Shall Not Die

Peter N. Muya

I SHALL NOT DIE
PETER N. MUYA

First edition. July 2024.

Second edition. June 2025

Copyright © 2025 Peter N Muya.

ISBN 9798227754523

All rights reserved.

For information contact Bishop Peter Muya via muyabishop@gmail.com

Phone: +254724805868/+254798649468

Edited by Peter Hinga Kiago. Email: quibpet3r@gmail.com

Phone: +254706488565

I dedicate this book to the youth and the children who are victims of drug and sex abuse.

It is very unfortunate that children find themselves living desperately in the streets in this hurting world. Many of them are languishing in hopelessness, not knowing where to turn for help. Children are engaging themselves in evil behaviors like sex abuse ,drug abuse and illicit brew consumption. I encourage the children by telling them to declare, "I SHALL NOT DIE." Never give up or lose hope.

"I am an ambassador of Christ. I am more than extraordinary;
I am what God says I am. I can do what God says I can."
T.L. Osborn

Foreword

IN THIS BOOK YOU WILL find a powerful message for the ministers of God, about how they should wake up with the gospel of truth to address the problems of sex abuse, drug abuse and alcoholism. They should give the hurting world hope for survival by releasing the word of God.

Peter Muya has a wonderful testimony of God's love upon his life after surrendering his miserable life to Jesus Christ, when he confessed that he was a drug addict and illicit brew abuser. God's love arrested him before he perished in hell forever. He was delivered; today he trusts in God's word to rescue victims of addiction from drug abuse. His submission to God's word caused his deliverance from addiction.

This book is a thrilling introduction of how you can be set free from drug abuse and alcoholism. It is in a series of self-harm. Copies should be given to elders, deacons, youth leaders, teachers, and the community to teach victims the biblical way of deliverance from drug abuse.

The author would like to teach the youth and anybody who would mind to listen about the effect of drug abuse and how you can be delivered. Clarity and passion are the distinguishing marks of Muya's book. This is one of the best undertakings on how to rescue the youth, children, and the community from drug abuse menace.

Through his ministry, the victims are changed by the powerful Word of God to become useful business people and good citizens.

If you are looking for a clear and simple doctrine of redemption from evil behaviors, here it is. Declare with him, "I shall not die."

The author should be supported to accomplish his vision of rescuing victims of drug abuse and alcoholism from premature death. May God give him more wisdom, grace, and favor as he ministers hope to the hopeless drug addicts in Kenya. The author's main objective is to rescue street children, the youth, and the society from drug abuse.

Victims do not know that addiction is a disease which is hard to treat. This evil habit has claimed many untimely deaths in our country. Yet many families are still wallowing in ignorance about drug abuse without knowing that their children are victims.

The truth is that many school children and college students are the highest abusers of drugs, and their parents are not aware. That's why the author started this campaign dubbed, I Shall Not Die. He is going around counseling, educating, informing pupils, students, street children, and the society about the dangers of drug addiction. Prevention is better than the cure. That's why he is helping the youngsters from ten through thirty-years old before it's too late.

Today he is advising students to avoid the first puff or sip. Students are becoming drug peddlers in secondary schools and colleges; they are selling miraa, bhang, alcohol, cigarettes, and even hard drugs like cocaine and heroine. Hats why the author is helping our young people before they suffer from depression or the problem of drug addiction which is called by doctor's drug-induced psychosis (DIP). This condition causes victims to commit suicide. Read this inspiring book and you will be delivered from drug abuse.

REV JAMES OSORO.

Acknowledgement

I WANT TO THANK MY friend, Mr. Sammy Kariuki, for doing all the typing of this manuscript and his wonderful suggestions on how to format it. Thank you my friend, editor Natalie, and Dr. Carol Wambui who helped me on my research on commonly abused drugs and their treatment. Special appreciation to the leaders of Christ Ordained Kids,a Community Based Organization for your moral support.

Introduction

"BHANG" IS THE MOST destructive drug in general use today in Kenya. Children and teenagers are increasingly drinking illicit brew. Bhang and alcohol have destroyed countless families children,,youth and have caused untimely deaths.

My research shows that students drink alcohol and abuse drugs to celebrate. Others use it so that they may feel relaxed. Others say they want to drown their troubles in the substance. In many cases students drink to show off. Others want to relieve their tensions or escape from reality. Others want to feel happy, but they don`t realize that drugs and alcohol are destroying their manhood or womanhood. We have an increase in drug abuse in both schools and colleges.

There is widespread use of hard drugs such as heroin, cocaine, marijuana and crack. In places where alcohol or drugs are sold, crime is very high. You will hear cases of rape, suicide, murder, as well as other crimes.

Drug abuse and alcohol consumption did much to deteriorate my physical body. In fact, drug abuse was altering the functioning of every organ in my body. Because I was a drug abuser and alcoholic, which made me develop high blood pressure. The doctors told me it could have increased the risk of developing stroke. I felt high and thought the whole world was in my hands. These evil behaviors led me to committing a variety of criminal activities.

"Why was I born?" I questioned myself. There appeared nothing special about me, a drug addict who hated and cursed his own life. My creditors marked me off as a bad debtor. My old pals avoided me like a dreaded disease. Then time came when liquor no longer eased my quaking body or calmed my enslaved mind. I was a complete wreck and a social misfit.

The worst thing that happened in my life was when I was involved in a very tragic road accident along the Nakuru-Nairobi highway near Mbaruk trading center. I was high when I was riding towards home, I was suddenly hit by a speeding lorry. I was rescued and taken to the hospital by a good Samaritan. He collected me on the roadside, bleeding on the ground after the accident in a near death condition. Thank God that when he took me to the hospital, the doctors saved my life. I survived death by a whisker.

The devil`s plan was to kill me before I repented my sins so that he could push me to hell. But God`s plan was to save me before I perished in hell and use me for His glory. My life was full of ups and downs when I remembered the near death experience; it reminded me that there was still light at the end of the dark tunnel of my life.

God spared my life for a reason, though I was not aware of it at the time. I was tired of living with all these evil behaviors, and I called Jesus Christ to save me from this miserable life of drug addiction. With every fiber of my being I called Jesus to save my life. I was saved and transformed. Today, I`m rescuing children, the youth and the community from drug abuse.

This book, I Shall Not Die, is about my motto or my campaign against the effects of drug abuse and alcoholism. We are rescuing children and the youth from sex and drug abuse through our registered [CBO] Christ Ordained Kids Organization based in Nakuru town.

CHAPTER ONE

TORMENTED BY DRUG ADDICTION

DRUG ABUSE AND ALCOHOL consumption did much to bring deterioration to my physical body. The doctors say long-term alcohol abuse causes an increased risk of cancer of the liver, stomach, and colon. Alcohol destroys thousands of irreplaceable brain cells after every drink. Wine and beer cause the lining of the stomach to become inflamed, often leading to the formation of peptic cancers.

Because I was a chronic abuser of alcohol and drugs, I developed high blood pressure, which the doctors told me would increase my risk of developing stroke and heart attack. In fact, drug abuse was altering the functioning of every organ in my body. As I felt high, I thought the whole world was in my hands. It led me to committing a variety of criminal activities.

Drug abuse and alcohol consumption has brought millions of deaths today in the world. Every day the traffic officers report the death toll. Alcohol and drug abuse are responsible for more hospital admissions than any other single cause. Many prisoners in jails are there because of alcohol or drug-related crimes.

I escaped death by a whisker, but I sustained many injuries and compound fractures in my body. That's why I want to put in your minds the picture of the harmful effects of drugs and alcohol. There are very high risks associated with drug and alcohol abuse. I started drinking as a social act. It was for fun. But after a time, I got hooked and became a frequent user. Although it had started with only occasional use of alcohol and drugs, I eventually became hooked into habitual use. I witnessed what alcohol did to the villagers, to my family, and to me. I encourage people to refuse the first-friendly drink.

Alcohol is the most destructive drug in general use today. In Kenya, alcoholism is one of our most serious national problems. Children and youth are increasingly drinking alcoholic beverages. Alcohol has destroyed countless families and has caused many untimely deaths. Students drink alcohol and abuse drugs to celebrate. Others use it so that they can feel relaxed, while others say they want to drown their troubles in the substance. In many cases, students drink to show off. Others want to relieve tensions or escape from reality. Others want to feel happy but don't realize that drugs and alcohol are destroying their youth.

We have an increase of drug abuse in both schools and colleges. There is a widespread use of hard drugs, such as heroin, cocaine, marijuana, and crack. In the places where alcohol or drugs are sold, crime is very high. You will hear cases of suicide as well as murder and other crimes.

In my home, at the age of ten years, every child displayed all of the symptoms of addiction. At the age of thirteen years, every child helped Mother sell chang'aa in the brew dens. As young boys, my brother and I were always sent to keep watch and signal when the policemen were approaching. Then we would be compensated with a glass of chang'aa. When my brother and I became teenagers, we were used by Mum to transport chang'aa into Nakuru Town using a bicycle.

I was drinking chang'aa at a tender age, smoking cigarettes, and abusing the locally grown drug known as bhang. They also called it cannabis sativa. After abusing this particular drug, I started experiencing some of the psychological effects of it. I abused drugs more and more, and these drugs had a chemical substance that interfered with my perception, my mood, and my consciousness. It had psychological effects in my life and caused problems with my heart. My heart started beating faster than usual. Although it helped me to withdraw from reality, it lessened fatigue and increased boldness, self-confidence, energy, and wakefulness.

One day I tried to study the stems, leaves, flowers, and seeds of this bhang plant that made me very high. The craving in me for this plant did not allow me to miss a single dose, and I did not find any solid fact that made me a slave to it. Abusers called it "weed."

For me, this plant had led me into a lust for women and girls. After abuse, I did not want to see anybody with a skirt. The drug stimulated my body with the lust of the eyes. That's why you will hear many cases of rape perpetrated by drug addicts. Some youth believe that drugs increase romance and sex desire. They claim that drugs induce fantasies that heighten sex in their lives. That's why they use drugs before any date. To others, drugs cause impotency.

So, be very careful because sometimes drugs can destroy your manhood or womanhood. Many youths have been destroyed by an overdose of drugs. And for me, drugs triggered a prickly sensation that increased enticing stories to ladies in love-making. That's why you could see young men in town staring at the big billboards that display shameful pictures of girls on commercial advertisements on the roadsides.

Other youths are addicted to pornography or erotic movies. That's why you hear of cases of masturbation as a result of drugs. Many youths become trapped in pornography websites on the Internet. After watching these filthy images, they become crazy sexually. Rape could be an option on how to deal with the organ of a man becoming sexually aroused. Others will opt to hire a prostitute to release their sexual desires.

The use of drugs and alcohol can cause an irresistible urge to have sex in the body of a young man. Although every man is born with hidden sexual desires, drugs overstimulated and trigger the desire. That's why many of those who sell alcohol in bars and clubs are women. If any man's desire is aroused, he can go to these maids, purchase them for a while, and after that continue drinking. That's why alcohol destroys families and increases the transmissions of HIV/AIDS throughout the whole world.

The Bible warns, "Do not desire her beauty in your heart and do not let her capture you with her eyelashes, for the price of prostitutes is only a loaf of bread but a married woman hunts down a precious life. Can a man carry fire next to his chest and his clothes not be burned? Or can one walk on hot coals and his feet not be scorched?" (Proverbs 6:25–28).

This warning is for those of us in bars and clubs. The lust for any woman by simply looking is immoral. Sex brings temporal satisfaction, but you may seriously regret the consequences. You will agree with me that alcohol and drug abuse increase sexual desires and HIV/AIDS transmissions.

In my days of drug abuse, I did not care. I would have any size of a woman without caring for the consequences. In those days, there were no stories of AIDS, so I would be cracking jokes with my friends by telling them that I wouldn't want to miss pleasures, paying taxes, or death. I believed that death was a solution to end all of my problems. Little did I know that the devil was destroying my life; that I was like a toy in his hands. The craving induced into my body led me to smoking cigarettes, too. It began as fun, but eventually I became hooked to it as well. The craving was deep in my blood and veins.

I have seen how smoking has led many people to the grave. Millions of smokers have been polluting our fresh air with poisonous chemicals, causing cancer, bronchitis, emphysema, and high blood pressure. It has caused millions of deaths, despite the warnings of the health hazards explained in commercials. Kenya has banned smoking in public places.

Many people smoke, making the multinational tobacco firms very rich by exploiting their health. They say that tobacco firms are employing many people, but on the other side, they are killing smokers.

As I write this book, many smokers are suffering from using tobacco for a long time. I'm advising smokers to find help from doctors in order to stop smoking because it is so dangerous for their health.

I will never forget how I was almost destroyed by the devil through evil addictions. I was crying helplessly without a comforter. I wished that I would die rather than live. For me, life was hopeless and meaningless. All of my labor to make me free was useless. My life was not certain; it was unpredictable. All of my problems were a heavy weight on my shoulders. I did not want to hear of anything concerning God or religion. I was in a pit and did not know how to get out of it.

I knew that I had been born and that one day I would die. At night I was disturbed by fearful dreams of death, and by day I contemplated death. I could not explain my deplorable condition to anybody. I had no peace of mind. My heart was full of anxiety and fear. My life was bound with chains that I could not see. My life was torn up like my trousers and shirt were. I was wearing worn-out shoes. I could not bathe for days because of hopelessness and depression.

I was angry about my life and angry with everybody. I thought everybody was against me. My family and relatives thought something must have been wrong with me; I could not concentrate or make simple decisions in life. I could not even plan on what to eat or wear.

It was a shattering experience suffering from such depression. Whenever I woke up in the morning, I felt a black cloud hovering over my life, and I was in an utter state of disappointment. My life was full of agony and misery. The fear of ending up in a mental hospital disturbed me. Because of drug abuse, my mind was not functioning properly. Sometimes sleeping was very difficult at night.

My family tried to help me, but I slipped and ploughed back into addictions. Stress was a constant disorder in my life. The gravity of my predicament made me think of committing suicide.

Sometimes friends came to visit me and found me laughing without cause. Laughing, but living in pain. I could not marry because no girl would accept me in this condition. I was suffering from joblessness and failures in life. I could not fulfill any of my expectations.

Today, I am seeing alcoholics and drug abusers suffering the way I once had. They are consuming illicit brews that are mixed with a very poisonous chemical substance called "methanol," which interferes with the organs in the body. It has caused many deaths. Victims are complaining of regular headaches, ulcers, nausea, heart problems, and high blood pressure.

There are many ills linked to the addiction of this illicit brew sold in the market. Families are always demonstrating to show the world dangers caused by abusing these illegal substances. Thousands of wives are complaining that their husbands are impotent in bed, as their manhood has been destroyed by these illicit brews. Millions of our youth are drowning in an evil sea of drugs addiction and alcoholism. Criminal activity is increasing in our society. Victims are suffering from the damaging consequences of addictions.

Drug and substance abuse gives the abusers an artificial source of well-being. The addicts call drugs "herbs." And the drugs cause them to suffer even more when they try to withdraw. Our youth are suffering physically, emotionally, and mentally.

God has given every human being the freedom to choose. You can choose life or death, blessings or curses (Deuteronomy 30:19). Many youths have chosen death. That's why I'm helping the youth today to choose life. I'm warning the youth by telling them that there is "death in the pot of the illicit brew."

I have volunteered to rescue the youth from drug addiction. I warn them not to be addicted to smoking cigarettes because the poisonous chemicals like nicotine, carbon monoxide, and others will get into their heart by passing through their blood and into their whole body. Users will start staggering; trembling with imbalance because of muscular paralysis. And when these chemicals pass through the lungs, you could develop lung, liver, and kidney cancers. It can also cause stomach ulcers, which could lead to death.

My message to everybody is that there is death in the pot of the illicit brew. Look for example at the people of central Rift Valley. They are blessed with very productive land, but instead of making use of their land, they are involving themselves with alcoholism and drug abuse. We have seen thousands of victims becoming blind or developing other vision problems. Others become impotent, while others engage in a lot of domestic violence at home.

I'm telling the youth that one day in Israel, people there were suffering with famine in the land. One of the sons of the prophet went out in the open field and brought herbs and wild vine. After cooking, they served the hungry, but while the people were eating, they all cried and said to the prophet, Elisha, "O' man of God, there is death in the pot" (2 Kings 4:38–41). When the prophet prayed, he destroyed the spirit of death in the pot.

That is why that today, as a former addict and now a servant of God, I am declaring that there is death in the pot! Stop abusing the herb and wild vine. God is against the herb and the wild vine because it causes death. Drug addicts and alcoholics invite poverty into their homes.

The Bible warns, "Woe to those who rise early in the morning that they may run after strong drinks that tarry late into the evening as wine inflames them" (Isaiah 5:11). The Bible warns the breweries that make different brands of liquor, "Woe to him who makes his neighbor drink. You pour out your wrath and make them drunk in order to gaze at their nakedness" (Habakkuk 2:15). The Bible also says, "...For the drunkard and the glutton shall come to poverty and drowsiness shall clothe a man with rags" (Proverbs 23:21).

One second-generation liquor brand is called "sting." Why? Because the Bible says it "stings like an adder and bites like a serpent" (Proverbs 23:29). Another brand is called "fighter" because it fights the victims physically, mentally, financially, and emotionally.

"Wine is a mocker, strong drink a brawler, and whoever is led astray by it is not wise" (Proverbs 20:1). Are you a victim who is led astray by wine? Call Jesus Christ today in your heart and you will be totally saved and transformed.

CHAPTER TWO

MY REDEEMER LIVES

I WAS BORN AND BROUGHT up in a poverty-stricken family. My father was employed as a casual worker in what they called "Good Hope Farm." A white settler known as Lieutenant Colonel Pearson owned the farm. He was a retired army officer who paid his workers very little money.

My parents were both alcoholics. They helped us survive by brewing and selling the illicit brew, Chang'aa, to the villagers. I become an alcoholic and a drug addict as I grew up in this toxic atmosphere.

Ever since I was a little boy, I have loved gifts. During Christmas, Pearson would gather all the children to his home and give them gifts. I remember getting a packet of sweets, biscuits, toys, and balloons. The gifts were wrapped with beautiful gift wrappings. We opened them at home, comparing who got what. Naturally, this ended up in a lot of petty fights. Looking back to those years, I miss those wonderful times in life.

As for all the employees, including my father, Pearson gave them four kilos of beef, two kilos of sugar, and a packet of tea leaves each. These were the annual gifts given for this occasion.

In our home, no matter what economic hardships my parents were experiencing at the time, Christmas dresses and shoes were bought for our sisters. For us boys, they bought us new shirts, shorts, and shoes. New clothes were a must during this season, and it was a ritual in every home in those days. Our parents were very busy trying to keep us happy during this season.

Our relatives, aunties, uncles, and grandparents, would visit us during the season with their gifts. They were not allowed to give us cash gifts because, at that time, we were not allowed to handle money. However, we had very little use for it anyway.

During this season, we would be related to see preachers coming to bring the gospel into our village. The choir sang the Christian carols. They welcomed us in the church, where they had activities with the theme of the birth of Jesus Christ.

Every person and every age group had their favorite ways of entertainment and their ideas on how to celebrate the season. When I grew up, I joined the young generation, and I was one of the organizers of discos in the area. We could invite at least one of the artists who could perform during the season.

To us, the young people, Christmas entertainments started quite early with the switching on of the disco lights to mark the start of the celebrations. We could celebrate from early December right through Christmas and until the New Year. Many youths took their first sip of alcohol or a puff of cigarette in December associated with all pleasures and celebrations.

Christmas was heralded by the sounds of tinkling jingles, neon signs, and disco lights attracting the youth and enticing them into spending a lot of money in the disco halls, which were identified by their huge advertising banners. This was commonly experienced during the festive season, and it made the real meaning of Christmas lost in all our hearts.

We started the celebrations by puffing several rolls of bhang. Unfortunately, whether or not other people could bear witness to it, beneath what I had considered the great joy of merrymaking and dating that filled my heart at that time, deep in my soul, I was hurting. In my soul, I was yearning for freedom from economic problems, life miscalculations, joblessness, hopelessness, and many sex-related issues. Despite the short-lived pleasures, fun, and entertainment, I was longing for freedom. I wanted liberation from all these crippling evil desires and bondage that held me captive no matter which way I turned.

Let me explain to you the curiosity and the anxiety with which I embraced one particular Christmas season. During the season, I could date and drink, and I was always high on drugs. When I woke up very early in the mornings, my head would be aching, and I would be trying to remember what messes I had made the previous day.

I was very frustrated with hangovers, and I had disturbing voices in my mind because of the disco music and its messages. I had severe headaches and blurred vision. I was celebrating Christmas, but I continued to face many problems during the season.

Together with my brother and sisters, we were involved in different messes as we spent much money on entertainment. Let me ask: can pleasures build a family?

People encouraged us by telling us that drinking was not harmful. Drinking and dancing were the cornerstones of the festive season. They both showed we were celebrating Christmas in the village in those days.

Pleasures and the desires of the flesh controlled our lives, but unfortunately, in these joyful celebrations of merrymaking, you could suddenly hear the sounds of weeping, crying, and moaning from our hurting souls during and after the festivities.

Our hurting souls were yearning for freedom from sins because we were wallowing in sin and suffering without knowing that the full price had already been paid for the gift of salvation. We were freely given a Christmas gift with a difference, Christmases that were fulfilling despite the circumstances in this life. Jesus Christ is our greatest Christmas gift. A Christmas gift which was given with the promises of God to set us free from all forms of sins and bondage.

Remember the words of the Lord Jesus said in John 10:11. He promised to be the good shepherd in our lives. Everyone in the world can fail, but God's promises will stand forever. How could we be serving in this crooked generation without His wonderful love and guidance in our lives? God gave us Jesus Christ, His son, as our greatest gift.

He is a good shepherd who loves and cares for His sheep. He pulled us out of the roaring lion's mouth in the darkness, and He leads us in His marvelous light. He found us, and He forgave our sins. His mercies endure forever. He now carries us daily through the way of life.

His loving and caring hands, day by day, make us eat peacefully in His green pastures. He cares for our needs, trials, and sorrows. He knows our walk even in the darkest night. He keeps us even when we are passing in the bush. On every rough road, He directs and gently guides us.

Because He also suffered, He can comfort us in all of our trials and temptations. He will never leave us nor forsake us. I will trust in Him in all the days of my life.

He knows my voice when I'm coming in and when I'm going out. He is the door through which any man can enter and be saved. Jesus is now seeking you, and He has worked for your salvation. He is our salvation, healing, and deliverance.

Today I like to wish people a Merry Christmas and a prosperous New Year. I appeal to all Christians around the world to dedicate Christmas to helping the needy.

I know many people will be celebrating together with us by giving what you have to those who don't have. This can be an exciting way of making merry with the needy who are suffering from different kinds of problems in their lives. Despite your hard economic trials, just do something for the needy. Let Christmas be a time of giving to the less fortunate in life.

It's God Himself who began this mission of giving when He gave us the best gift, His only begotten son, more than two thousand years ago. The important gift to the needy is to help them receive Jesus Christ as their personal savior. However, as the word of God says, salvation is a free gift for us because God has already paid the price for it.

As we focus on this great gift that is given to us, let us focus on the spirit of goodwill and volunteer to help the needy. This is not a time to complain about the things we don't have in life, but rather it is our time to give the little we have to the needy.

Jesus came to get a job done; to save a lost and dying world. That is what Christmas is all about: the season when the Savior of the world was born! I have started a ministry for the needy. God cares about the needs of His people and the troubling situations in which they live!

When the angel told Mary of the miracle to come, Mary asked, "How shall this be?" The angel spoke faith to her. "With God, nothing shall be impossible." This is true even in your life. (Read Luke 1:26, 38)

Praise God! Try to imagine that it is Christmas once again, the time of the year when Christians all over the world celebrate the birth of Jesus Christ. During any year when we focus on this season of goodwill, we need to reflect on our lives and appreciate what we had achieved that year despite all the tragedies and problems that have hit our country of Kenya. This is not a time to moan, but rather a time to be happy that we had lived to see another Christmas. It is a time to show our love to all mankind and extend the spirit of goodwill beyond our homes. Let us take the Christmas mood to the needy and shout together with them, "Merry Christmas!"

Let us celebrate together with the needy because the Bible says, "For unto us a child is born, unto us a son is given and his name shall be called the wonderful counselor, the mighty God, the everlasting father, the prince of peace!" (Isaiah 9:6).

The prophet, Isaiah, had said, "The Lord himself will give you a sign, behold a virgin shall conceive and bear a son, and shall call his name Emmanuel" (which means, "God with us") (Isaiah 7:14).

God did what the prophet had said. God sent the angel, Gabriel, to Nazareth, a town in Galilee, to a man, Joseph, a descendant of David.

The virgin's name was Mary. The angel went to her and said, "Greetings! You are highly favored! The Lord is with you. The Holy Spirit will come upon you, and the power of the Most High will overshadow you. So, the holy one to be born will be called the son of God" (Luke 1:26, 35).

God showed His greatest love to us by giving us His only begotten son. As the Bible says, "For God so loved the world that he gave his only begotten son, that whoever believes in him should not perish, but have everlasting life" (John 3:16).

This is what Christmas means; it is to celebrate the birth of our Lord and Savior, Jesus Christ. As we focus on this great gift that God gave to mankind, we should appreciate what Jesus did on the cross for our sins. This is not the time to live in sin and its pleasures, but rather it is a time to receive the greatest gift, which was sent to us by the living God. We are to receive eternal life in Jesus Christ as we shout, "Merry Christmas."

It is a time to show the love of God to every creature on Earth and extend the spirit of goodwill to the needy. Christmas should be a time of giving because God Himself had always demonstrated His love towards us when we were still sinners (Romans 5:8).

After accepting Christ through the ministry of Billy Graham in 1978, I joined the ministry a few years later as a full-time evangelist. Two years later, I was chosen as a full-time pastor in a local church in Gilgil. I had been serving God in different local churches before starting my ministry in the year 2000.

Gospel Messengers Church was founded with the objective of taking the gospel out to the people in the crowded places of life, such as city centers, marketplaces, racecourses, fairgrounds, bus stations, railway stations, open-air streets, and the coast. We have many full-time evangelists who spend most of their time out in the open-airs preaching the gospel. We also have many full-time pastors who oversee local churches in cities, towns, and the villages.

I am a full-time pastor, but I like to be involved in evangelism and also spend much time traveling all over this country to teach the Word in the local churches and preach the gospel in the open-airs.

My vision is: "reaching the unreached and giving hope to the hopeless." My commission is: "preach the gospel." My mission is: "Woe to me if I do not preach the gospel." And my motto is:" I Shall Not Die" God called me to rescue children from drug abuse.

Sinners are in my prayers; "Revive us, Lord!" I want the Lord to tell me, "I was hungry, and you gave me food. I was thirsty, and you gave me a drink. I was a stranger, and you took me in; I was naked, and you clothed me. I was sick, and you visited me. I was in prison, and you came to see me" (Matthew 25:35, 36).

I had started a Faith Ministry in my church. Its aims and purposes are to sensitize children and the community on their rights against the current predicaments facing society, among them being HIV/AIDS, poverty, drug abuse, alcoholism, prostitution, and child abuse. We are reaching young people in schools and colleges through songs, poems, dramas, and sharing the gospel.

As a church ministry, our moral obligation is to assist in the fight against drug abuse and HIV/AIDS pandemics in Kenya. We, therefore, network with all our local churches and conduct HIV/AIDS training on life skills and HIV/AIDS prevention programs.

Giving to the needy could be a wise way to celebrate Christmas. Many people would be planning to save money, which they would spend during the holiday on the coast or in their rural homes where they would be celebrating with loved ones, relatives, and friends. Others would be celebrating by eating their favorites: mutton and beef. Others would be celebrating by giving and receiving gifts from friends and loved ones.

But, remember! All the gifts that you can receive in this world could be useless. The greatest gift to us is Jesus, Emmanuel. Jesus is the only gift that lasts forever. All other gifts in the world will eventually perish and be forgotten. But, Jesus lives forever. Why don't you accept this wonderful and everlasting gift that God has given to us now? Jesus is here to save you and meet you at the point of your need!

Remember. When you are celebrating Christmas by abusing drugs or drinking beer or by dating, you are committing sins, and you are acting against the Word

of God. Remember that while you are enjoying and celebrating in whichever way you choose; many hurting souls are suffering from nothing to eat. Some are in great pain in a hospital bed, and some are facing different problems in their lives. "Who shall separate us from the love of Christ? Shall tribulations or distress or persecution or famine or nakedness or peril or sword?" (Romans 8:35).

By the grace of God, some individuals, non-governmental organizations, and well-wishers have sent their gifts to the community director, "Gospel Messengers Church."

My appeal to organizations is to dedicate their resources to supporting needy kids or those who are less fortunate. I know that ministry to the needy kids' costs, but it touches the heart of God to release an enormous reward or blessing to all those who minister to kids.

As the Bishop of Gospel Messengers Church I was surprised when I visited one of our pastors, Rev Joram, in his church in Nakuru city. I saw him opening big boxes packed with small boxes full of gifts donated to small kids by Samaritan Purse, a charitable organization of Billy Graham. He introduced me the regional office and they agreed to put our church in Kiambogo village, Elementaita, Gilgil Sub County in their list to get the gifts for kids. God bless this organization that ministers hope to little kids in many churches in Kenya. We are called to preach the gospel to kids.

All I can say to all those who are helping us to reach kids by extending the spirit of goodwill with gifts to kids is a very big "Thank you!" "Yet in all these things we are more than conquerors through Him who loved us" (Romans 8:37).

The Bible says, "The wages of sin is death, but the gift of God is eternal life in Christ Jesus, Our Lord" (Romans 6:23). We are very committed to introducing kids to Jesus, for He is the greatest gift to us all. Today this great gift is still offered. What will you say before the throne of God at the Judgment Day after you had refused this great Christmas gift that is offered by God?

Will you accept the gift and inherit eternal life? Or, will you reject it to inherit death or everlasting destruction? The decision is yours now! Jesus Christ is the only lover! In this world, just say, "Yes," to Jesus.

I wish you a very happy and prosperous life. This could be a message of hope to the hopeless, the needy, and the less fortunate from "The Gospel Messenger" who is "living for Christ."

To many, the mention of Christmas brings the visions of shopping, visiting, and decorating of glittering Christmas trees with balloons tied on every side. To others, it means celebrating by eating cakes, sweets, and having fun.

But as for me, I believe Christ is always within me, so I celebrate Christmas every day of my life. My suggestion to you before you think to celebrate Christmas is first to receive Jesus as your personal savior in your troubled heart, as this will bring the true meaning of Christmas into your life. Don't just take Christmas as merely a religious activity or festival. Think about the true reason for this season.

As a Christian, I'm conscientious about Christmas and don't want to be among the people who call themselves Christians but are actually doing all sorts of evil things because of celebrating Christmas. I'm self-controlled in my life as I focus on the subject of Christmas. I don't want to be carried by the mood of Christmas that I'm not able to explain.

In my life, the best and most important message is about Christmas. I like to hear how Jesus was born, grew up, and died on the cross for my sins and all the sins of the world.

You may have many reasons and conceptions as to why you celebrate Christmas. However, remember that Jesus Christ is the only reason for Christmas. Without Him in your soul, you cannot enjoy Christmas and Christmas is meaningless.

Christmas should not be a time of feasting and merrymaking. It should be a time to rejoice that our sins will never lead us to eternal doom and separation from our Holy God.

I have a message of Love for you that during Christmas, a holy and exalted Son of God was born to save us from our sins, sorrows, iniquities, and transgressions. "By His stripes, we are healed" (Isaiah 53:4–5).

Jesus left His father's glory and splendor to become a man so that He could feel our pains, and, having done all, He took our sins upon Himself, offering to suffer and die for us all. He comes to reconcile us back to God. Why should we reject Him as our personal Savior? By receiving Him into your heart, you are accepting the message of Christmas.

To me, Christmas has a special meaning, and I observe it while contemplating the needs of others. Apart from celebrations, I have to take my time to help and visit the less fortunate and the needy people in our society. Visiting the needy in hospitals or nursing homes and sharing with them the word of God is a fulfilling ministry in my life.

It's good to share food, clothes, and even the word of God with the needy. To me, Christmas is not a one-day activity because "Jesus is the same yesterday, today, and forever" (Hebrews 13:8). Jesus is a gift for you for all times.

I like visiting the needy kids to celebrate and have fun with them during Christmas. They appreciate me as they walk over shoulder-high to meet me. Kids love Christmas, and every year they long for it to come. I'm happy to tell them the true significance of Christmas: Jesus is my redeemer; my redeemer lives.

CHAPTER THREE

RESCUING CHILDREN FROM DRUG ABUSE

HAVING A HUMBLE BEGINNING myself, I can identify with the street children who have engaged themselves in drug abuse menace. I will never forget how I was horrified to learn the unnatural and miserable conditions these hopeless street children are living in, especially the girl-child. In Kenya street children are commonly known as "Chokora" or "chucks."

"Do not weep!" I encouraged Moni, a young street girl who was found weeping in the streets of Nakuru city after she was repeatedly raped by a gang of street boys. She had joined others in the streets after she was disowned by her single mother who lived in the Ghetto. She started a very miserable life of surviving by begging stranger's money and abusing all the types of illicit drugs, including glue and petrol.

Her story shocked my perspective, and when I shared with Dr. Kwake and Rev. Joram, they appointed me as the patron in their registered organization, "Christ ordained kids." A community based organization, under the ministry of labor and social protection.

Our main objective was to rescue these street kids from drug abuse, pick-pocketing, rape, burglary, and robbery with violence before they become victims of insecurity in the city.

Giving them food, clothing or shelter is not enough; they needed to be given skilled training to equip them to be self-reliant. Also, they must be guided to a well of compassion, salvation and deliverance in Jesus Christ before it's too late. I Shall Not Die is a book about how these street children rescue team is wiping away tears from their eyes and how they are turning their weeping into inexpressible joy. Partner with us and help us in making a difference in their hurting lives. With God everything is possible.

This book is a voice of hope to the hopeless especially street children, vulnerable kids and orphans. You will get page turning and inspiring information that will make you want to read more. Watch out for the much anticipated release of two latest books from the series of inspiring hope! Namely, Never Lose Hope and Hope for Survival. My redeemer lives, so do not weep again. Call Jesus Christ to deliver you from your sins, evil behaviors and addictions.

No one plans to become an orphan. Things and events happen in life without expectation. Some children are orphaned when they are very young, and others are orphaned when they are old enough to know their parents. The Bible says, "A father to the fatherless, a defender of widows is God in His Holy dwelling"(Psalms 68:5).

The Bible warns, "Do not take advantage of a widow and an orphan. If you do, they cry out for me, I will certainly hear their cry, and I will kill you with the sword, you will become widows and your children fatherless" (Exodus 22:22–24).

The Bible says, "Religion that God our Father accepts as pure and faultless is this: to look after orphans and widows in their distress..." (James 1:27).

Some orphans had only lost one parent, while others had lost both parents. When orphans know their parents are dead, they grow up in mental and emotional torture. Orphans need parental care and guidance. That care and counseling are some of the things we are providing in our ministry to the orphans.

Orphans feel good when they are eating together with people who love and appreciate them. God is helping us to encourage the orphans; loving them, providing for them, fellowship with them, praying with them, and, more importantly, appreciating them.

To all children, the Bible says, "Sons are a heritage from the LORD; children are an award from Him" (Psalms 127:3). All children are gifts from heaven. This includes the orphaned.

I lost my father, sister, and a brother. I know how to heal the brokenhearted, especially orphans who have lost both parents. I know the suffering they experience from extreme emotional problems.

God called me purposely to give hope to the hopeless and the brokenhearted. I have helped orphans recover from suffering, stress, depression, mental problems, frustrations, and other emotional problems. I know the sorrow, grief, and pain one experience after losing a loved one.

For some orphans, this pain takes a long time to heal, while in others, it takes a shorter time. The worst pain any human being can experience is the pain that ignites from the death of a loved one. Every orphan has his or her own unique pain.

I have heard different stories told by orphans. I try to heal their emotional tears by using the Word of God. The orphan feels lonely after the loss of his or her parents. However, I have tried to help them devote themselves fully to serving the Lord instead of following the world. Knowing Jesus is the best way to soothe some of the pain of losing parents.

Orphans are changing, and some of them are now helping me in the ministry. I have given them tips on how to overcome sorrow, grief, and pain. I teach them to accept the reality of their loss and of Jesus's love for them.

Through much prayer and regular counseling, I have helped many recover from trauma. Orphans should be given love and parental care. They need to know Jesus Christ personally and have a relationship with Him.

Some orphans suffer because their families are very selfish and greedy when sharing land or properties that their parents had left for them. The Bible says, "The poor are shunned even by their neighbors, but the rich have many friends" (Proverbs. 14:20).

When I married my wife, she was a teacher in the village school, and I noticed she had a ministry of hope and love for kids, and especially to the orphans.

I introduced her to my ministry. Today, she is helping me minister to orphans and vulnerable children. Some of these kids are HIV/AIDS victims. She would gather orphans and vulnerable children in one class and encourage them by singing songs and reading Bible stories to them every Friday.

My wife also welcomed them into our church services, where she introduced them to other children as she taught them the Word of God. She helped many overcome low esteem, anger, hopelessness, and disappointments in their lives.

The key word is, "Do not weep" (Luke 7:13). Jesus was encouraging a widow in the city of Nain after she had lost her beloved son. Jesus helped her by raising her son from death.

Children in our local church love attending Sunday school services, so we started a follow-up program of visiting their homes and families. Many families joined the church through this ministry to young children.

My wife, Mary, leads many souls to Christ through this ministry. Jesus is a wonderful counselor, Mighty God, Everlasting Father, and Prince of Peace (Isaiah 9:6).

Many kids are saved, delivered, and healed as they had received inner peace after beginning their eternal relationship with Jesus Christ.

Mary's ministry is centered on sincere devotion to preaching and ministering to young kids. Deeply etched in her heart is the suffering of young kids. Preaching to them and ministering to their physical needs became an integral part of her ministry.

I supported her in this vital ministry in our church. Mary said that even though her ministry is small in the village and not well known, it reflects Jesus' love for the children well. Jesus loves children, and Mary emulated Jesus in His loving and caring for children. She asks other people to help them, too.

Mary helps these children to think positively, be themselves, live by faith, and learn to overcome evil thoughts that could bring fear and doubts into their lives. She encourages them with the word of God, "Weeping may endure for a night, but joy comes in the morning" (Psalms 30:5).

In today's fast-paced society, there are many cases of defilement to small girls, a fact which has greatly hindered and threatened the education of female children in Africa. Mary is an advocate for young girls and young boys in Africa. She attends local and international meetings on torture against kids. She represents the orphans and the vulnerable children whose parents have died of HIV/AIDS or other causes.

Small children are often left alone to care for themselves and for their siblings. These hopeless kids are left suffering. They need food, shelter, health care, clothing, and education. Some of these kids fled their homes because of being neglected by their families. Many have gone to seek refuge on the streets, forcing them to engage in crime for survival.

Mary is locating a plot of land where she intends to build a big home for these hopeless children. A place where she can care for their physical as well as their spiritual needs.

She intends to employ a few social workers to help her in this ministry to children. She is asking the church members, neighbors, and other well-wishers to support her. She lost her mother and a brother-in-law. She knows the pain these young kids are experiencing in their lives.

Mary goes from house to house in the village to find kids who are not going to school and takes them to school. Will you be willing to support this ministry with the kids? Every year, Mary prepares a Christmas meal for them and gives them small gifts. She loves and appreciates each and every child.

"Do not weep!" is a campaign to encourage widows, orphans, the hurting, the hopeless, and the brokenhearted. This book was written with the purpose of bringing healing and restoration to victims of sorrow, pain, frustrations, and grief during crises. You will read true stories from the Bible to help you overcome stress and depression. The Scriptures will help to revive you and rekindle the fading flame of hope in your life.

That's why I minister hope to the victims of circumstances. No one who puts his or her faith in God is ever hopeless.

No matter how many times you have tried something without success, try it with Jesus Christ. You will find inner peace and rest for your soul. Tell Jesus all of your problems, burdens, sins, and diseases, and your weeping will be over. Remember how He comforted the widow in Nain? "Do not weep," He told her, and her son was resurrected. He can resurrect everything in your life. So, stop weeping. Do not be stuck in your hopelessness, sins, addictions, anxiety, stress, depression, or grief. Salvation is at hand.

After reading this book, I'm sure the Holy Spirit will minister hope, love, peace, healing, and restoration in your troubled life. You will learn lessons on counseling techniques, which will become a source of your healing. The Bible says, "Weeping may endure for a night, but joy comes in the morning" (Psalms 30:5).

May Jesus set you free from your sins and bondage. In the depth of your hurt, grief, pain, or sorrow, Jesus can change your spiritual death to eternal life.

I have helped many victims to recover from very harsh circumstances. Instead of weeping, you can declare, "I can do all things through Christ who strengthens me" (Philippians 4:13). Do not weep; there is hope for your survival. With God, all things are possible.

We have several empowering seminars for widows and orphans. We encourage them not to be victims but rather victors on the battlefield. We give them spiritual, physical, and emotional support.

We are teaching them how they can start income-generating programs. Times have changed. The days of going to school and getting a university education do not guarantee you a job. You need a good business plan for starting a small business with whatever you have and wherever you are.

Remember. Lucrative business comes from simple ideas. Everyone has an idea. Some are big ideas, while others are small ideas. You must have your own money-making ventures.

One orphan, named Kiptoo, was a drug addict. When he accepted Jesus Christ as his personal Savior, he became totally transformed. Kiptoo was brought into our empowering seminar by a friend. He learned simple ways to start a business. He started a small business in the Kongasis Trading Center in Elementaita, Gilgil. With KSh of 1,000, he started selling used empty cereal-bags. A few months later, his business was thriving fast because he did exactly what he had learned to do in our training. The young man managed to start in a market full of opposition. Later, he bought a plot of land and built his own house.

Listen. Business and entrepreneurship are about being able to see an opportunity and making it a business that is going to provide you with profit at the end of the day.

One widow, a single mother of eight children in Kaptembwa Estate of the town, Nakuru, was selling the illicit brew known as chang'aa in the estate. When she heard the gospel in a crusade, she was saved, healed, and transformed. Other widows brought her into our empowering seminar, where she was encouraged and empowered. She used the little money she had to start selling vegetables to her neighbors in the estate. Her faith was strengthened by attending church services. By a few years later, she had enough money to support her family and bought a plot in the estate.

The author of this book is an experienced counselor and a teacher of the Word. Widows and orphans have been finding healing through believing the Word of God and by acting upon the promises of God. They are set free! He ministers to the soul, body, and spirit. You will discover how to heal your soul by making the right decision to accept Jesus Christ as your savior and believing His word.

Whether you are feeling broken or downtrodden, you can be totally healed and restored by Jesus Christ through your faith.

Are you feeling lonely, restless, stressed, anxious, or depressed? Are you wounded or hurt emotionally, spiritually, or physically? Call Jesus Christ to save, deliver, and heal you now. Let me encourage you. "Weeping may endure for the night, but joy comes in the morning" (Psalm 30:5). "Do not weep," Jesus told the weeping widow of Nain (Luke 7:11:13).

We are reaching hopeless street kids for Christ. We are helping them to become shining Christians for the kingdom of God. We are aware of the fact that in Africa, traditionally, children have no value. However, Jesus loves and cares for every child in this world. The steadfast love of God to children never ceases; it is new every morning. God is calling us to do something by reaching these helpless kids with the gospel.

If you were to visit most of our cities in Africa, you would be horrified to see hundreds of small kids begging in the streets. Some of their parents died of HIV/AIDS, leaving them with relatives who have continued to increase the tension in their lives. Some of these are kids who have been disowned by their impoverished parents. With the spirit of rejection from their homes, they end up in the streets trying hard to survive by feeding on the leftover food in rubbish heaps and dustbins. At night you will see them sleeping in the streets covering themselves with dirty rags.

These kids suffer because they have no control over their fate. These unnatural circumstances lead them to abuse and injury. This problem forces the boys to engage in drugs, pickpocketing, burglary, and robbery with violence.

We are trying to help these kids. The first thing we do is approach them. Secondly, we try to talk to them positively and try to get them out of their terrible situations. Lastly, we encourage and counsel them. We have discovered that some are responding positively, while some are very violent because of drug abuse. They are fed up with life. When their misery, frustration, and hopelessness become severe, they come to believe that their only option is to commit suicide.

Even though some of these kids feel they have no hope of ever living a normal life, they can be rescued and live happy, fulfilling, and useful lives. We are called to show practical love and to break the spirit of rejection in their lives. We are to help these hopeless kids start new lives through Jesus Christ. Some of these children are living better lives now because of these efforts.

Many young people are living like beasts or oxen. Although they are human beings, their actions leave much to be desired. The cities are in the hands of demon-inspired youth, who drag the world into degradation and domination. These are the signs of a crooked generation, as well as the fulfillment of end-time prophecies. Something important is missing in the life of mankind. We are living in a most mysterious universe.

The Bible says, "Pure and genuine religion in the sight of God the Father means caring for orphans and widows in their distress and refusing to let the world corrupt you" (James 1:27). We have counseling programs for these kids; vocational and literacy training. We have a consuming zeal to help them.

There is a driving force in our spirits, as well as a fire that cannot be quenched, to minister to these needy kids. We are messengers of the gospel of love. We need to stop floundering around being generally preoccupied with other agendas. We are to instead move in faith and respond to the cries of the orphans and street children.

We are in the rehabilitation business bringing about personal change in the lives of these suffering kids in Africa. Together with Jesus Christ, we have started a rehabilitation process, which is powerful and unique. We are changing these kids from the inside-out and from the outside-in.

A change in behaviors begins with a change in the heart. We are to rescue the worst young criminals away from the grip of the devil and help them become a new creature in Christ. We have this unique, life-changing project in our ministry.

We are willing to be involved in the vital rehabilitation business of bringing about personal change in the lives of desperate kids. We are going to reach hopeless kids for Christ. We are going to make them shining Christians in the community. In Africa, children sometimes have no value, but in the kingdom of God, children are precious. Jesus loves and cares for every child in the world. The steadfast love of Jesus toward children never ceases. His compassion for children is new every morning. That's why Jesus is calling us to reach these hopeless kids with the gospel of love.

We are called to care for the hundreds of small kids who are begging in the streets. At night you will find these kids sniffing glue together and then sleeping together in the open streets with only an old rag for a covering. Diseases and cold torment them. They are chronically undernourished, as they don't have access to a healthy diet.

These kids suffer because they have no control over their fate. These unnatural circumstances lead them to abuse and injury to themselves and to others. These problems cause the boys to engage in drug abuse, pick-pocketing, burglary, and robbery. Many are violent. This is the reason why juvenile crime is rampant in our towns and cities.

I am trying to mobilize our local churches to help these kids come out from these unnatural circumstances and live a life that is fulfilling. We must help them as the Bible says and make them useful Christians in society. We are in a rehabilitation process that is unique and very effective. We are called into the ministry to look upon the needy through the eyes of Jesus Christ. The Bible says, "You have been a refuge for the poor, a refuge for the needy in their distress, a shelter from the storm and a shade from the heat" (Isaiah 25:4).

I am willing to leave my comfort zone to go out to where the hurting people are. By caring for these kids, their hearts will be softened to receive the gospel. We are an evangelical ministry that is concerned with meeting the physical, emotional, mental, and spiritual needs of these kids. "The Lord is a shelter for the oppressed, a refuge in times of trouble" (Psalms 9:9).

We are obeying the Word, which says, "Learn to do good, relieve the oppressed, defend the fatherless and plead for the widows" (Isaiah 1:17). We must be moved by compassion, which will make us break all cultural barriers as we move through the streets, slums, and ghettos to rescue these hurting souls.

Just for a moment, try to put yourself in these kids' shoes. I know you will do something about them. Let's lead these kids to sustainable development before it is too late. We must have counseling programs for these children. I have a consuming desire to help them. A change of behavior begins with a change of heart. Let's rescue these kids from the grip of the devil. Join us in this life-changing project.

Our ministry is planning to sponsor street kids those who are willing to return to school. Some were living in the slum areas where the parents could not afford to pay school fees for their children in school. We are moved by compassion as we see these bright students in the streets begging. We are aspiring to ignite the dream of education in the lives of these needy students.

Could you join us in sponsoring one or more of these desperate students who are loitering the streets? They need your help, encouragement, and comfort. Why not ask yourself, "What can I do to help these needy students?" If you are looking for something significant and life-changing to do with your money, consider sponsoring a needy student in the streets. Jesus said, "Whoever receives one of these little children in my name receives me; and whoever receives me, receives not Me but Him who sent me" (Mark 9:37).

Remember. A penniless student needs a caring friend to help him or her succeed. You can sponsor a student, or at least ask for the details on how to sponsor a needy student. God had unconditional love for us even when we were still sinners in this world. Shouldn't we extend that love to the needy children? If you sponsor a student, he or she will pray for you, love you, and embrace you. We are willing to connect you with a student in need. Why don't you promise to make a difference for one hurting student?

We are soon starting a program that will be offering vocational training in tailoring, carpentry, Jua Kali workshops, and computer courses for the street kids and underprivileged youth in the slum areas. After the course, the participants would be assisted through small-scale microfinance revolving loans so that they can develop their own businesses.

They will be mentored on how to market their products. The participants will be generating income to support themselves and meet their basic needs. Some of these youths are learning how to plant tree nurseries and sell the trees to farmers. We are also teaching them the Word of God.God is supplying all of their needs according to His riches in glory. We are looking up to God, the one who loves kids. We pray and intercede for the kids and widows, asking Him to guide them.

Please, promise to support this noble ministry of needy kids with your treasures and with your prayers. God of the kids will bless you.

CHAPTER FOUR

GIVING HOPE TO THE VULNERABLE CHILDREN

GOD IS MOVING AS NEVER before in the lives of women pastors. He is moving mightily in the life of Pastor Mary Njoroge. Mary became a Christian in Magomano High School, Nyandarua. After completing her college, she became a teacher in the village primary school. That's when she met her beloved husband, a pastor in the village church. After four years in a serious relationship, they were joined in holy matrimony.

Mary struggled to preach the gospel to pupils in the school, so she ministered to vulnerable children and orphans. Some of the children had HIV/AIDS. Mary read the Bible stories in her class to encourage children to be saved through Christ. She read the Bible stories to encourage people living with HIV/AIDS to overcome fear, anxiety, stress, doubts, low self-esteem, frustration, anger, depression, hopelessness, and disappointment in their hurting lives. "Do not weep," she read (Luke 7:13).

Mary led many to Jesus Christ, the wonderful counsel and mighty God, Everlasting Father, and Prince of Peace. Children were saved and delivered as they received inner peace in their troubled hearts.

When local church leaders reviewed Mary's ministry to the children, she was appointed as a pastor to the children. She was leading more than 100 children in one Sunday school class. Deeply etched in her life is the suffering of small children. Preaching and ministering to the needs of hopeless children became an integral part of her ministry.

Her dear husband supported her in this vital ministry in the church. Mary believes that even though her ministry seems very small in the eyes of villagers, it reflects Jesus's love to the children. She emulates Jesus in loving and caring for children. Her campaign to children is called "I Shall Not Die."

She helps children think positively, obey their parents/teachers, and be themselves. She teaches them to live by faith and to overcome the lusts of the flesh. Children are taught how to overcome evil thoughts that could bring fear and doubts in their lives. They taught them how to avoid sinful behaviors.

The Bible says, "Weeping may endure for a night, but joy comes in the morning" (Psalm 30:5). Mary is also an advocate for a girl child in Africa. In today's fast-paced society, there are many cases of defilement in small girls, a fact which has greatly hindered and threatened the education of the girl children in Africa.

She loves to minister to the orphans and vulnerable children whose parents have died of HIV/AIDS or other causes. Children are left alone to care for themselves and their siblings. These suffering children need:

- Food
- Shelter
- Health care
- Clothing
- Education

Some of these children seek refuge on the streets, where they are forced into crime in order to survive. Mary is locating a plot where she can build a home and a church for the believers and the small children; a home where children can come for home-based care, spiritual counseling, and other basic needs. She is asking some volunteers to assist her with the young kids in her ministry. She is asking volunteers to help her to go from house to house to encourage needy children to go to school and bring them to the church to be helped.

Mary has devoted herself and her ministry to children, orphans, and vulnerable kids. She is asking friends, well-wishers, and neighbors to assist her in making her vision to help young kids a reality.

Every year she prepares a meal during Christmas and shares it with children in the village. She is nicknamed "Mum" by the children. Your support with any amount of money would help greatly—partner with her in giving hope for the survival of the hopeless children. God bless you!

My vision is to minister to hurting kids. I pray for them and ask them to pass near me so that I can touch their heads and declare blessings into their lives. I am a minister of the gospel.

"Do not weep" is my message to the hurting kids. I help them to overcome fear, anxiety, stress, doubts, low self-esteem, frustrations, anger, depression, hopelessness, and disappointment in their hurting lives.

I lead troubled kids to Jesus Christ so they can know Him personally. Many have found peace, joy, and hope in their hearts. I know that Jesus loves children. As a bishop, I'm supporting my vision. I intend to locate a plot where I want to build a home for kids known as "Messengers Children's Home."

Deeply etched in my heart I can sense the suffering of small kids. They call me "Guka," which means "grandfather." Preaching hope and ministering love to hurting children has become an integral part of my ministry.

My wife supports my important ministry. My ministry may seem small in your eyes, but it reflects Jesus Christ, the greatest lover of kids. I emulate Jesus Christ by caring and loving needy kids. I am helping children to live positively by God's grace, as well as to overcome peer pressure and youthful lusts. Together with the ECD teacher Mr. Kuto of Kanorero village in Elementaita ward, Gilgil, we are making great strides in our organization, stay up Rehabilitative Community Based Organization in giving hope to the hopeless and vulnerable children.

Please support this survival vision. God bless you. I am also an advocate of vulnerable kids in Africa. I am protecting young kids from child abuse and female genital mutilation. I minister to kids whose parents have died of HIV/AIDS. I believe children should be given food, shelter, healthcare, clothing, and education.

I am rescuing young girls from defilement and early marriages in Africa. That's why I want to build a home for hurting children where they can find shelter, refuge, spiritual counseling, and other basic needs. I am asking donors, friends, well-wishers, and NGOs to assist in making my vision a reality.

I would very much appreciate any amount of money that the Lord can lead you to give. Partner with us in providing hope for survival to these hurting children.

The Bible encourages me to serve God in my ministry to the hopeless and the hurting. "For the gifts and the calling of God are irrevocable" (Romans 11:29). I am using my gifts to fulfill my call, just as God had called upon Moses to deliver the Israelites from bondage and slavery from the king pharaoh. During Joseph's lifetime, the Egyptians treated the people of Israel kindly. But after

Joseph died, a king who cared nothing for Israelites began to rule Egypt.

The king was afraid that the Israelites would become too numerous and powerful. He ruled over them harshly, and he commanded all baby boys of Israelites to be killed. However, God's ways are different from man's ways. He planned how He was to save His people, the Israelites, from the bondage and slavery of the Egyptians.

At this crucial time, a lovely boy was born to an Israelite family. For a while, his mother hid him, but soon she made plans to save him from the Egyptians. God provided a way to save this child from death. The mother made a little basket from weeds that grew by the river. She covered it with pitch to keep out the water. Then she put her baby into the basket and placed it at the edge of the river. She sent her twelve-year-old daughter, Miriam, to keep watch of the baby.

God sent the pharaoh's daughter and her maids to where they would find the basket by having them go down to the river to bathe. The princess sent one of her maids to get the basket. When she opened it, the little baby began to cry. "This is an Israelite baby," the princess exclaimed. She loved him at first sight.

Miriam, who was watching them at a distance, came and asked the princess if she could get a Hebrew woman to help in nursing the baby for the princess. The princess agreed, and Miriam ran to get her mother.

When she brought her mother, the princess happily gave her the child, and she promised to pay for his upkeep. When the child was old enough to leave his mother, the princess took him into her own home in the palace and named him Moses.

Moses grew among the Egyptians and learned their ways of doing things, along with their wisdom. But deep in his heart, he was planning on how he could save his people from Israel from bondage and slavery.

In Egypt, the Israelites worshipped and prayed to God to save them. The Egyptians worshipped idols and animals. The Bible says that Moses enjoyed all the privileges, rights, opportunities, and benefits of the son of a king. But deep in his heart, he felt the call of God to save his people, the Israelites, from bondage and slavery. "By faith Moses, when he came of age, refused to be called the son of Pharaoh's daughter, choosing rather to suffer affliction with the people of God than to enjoy pleasures of sins for a season"(Hebrews 11:24–25).

Moses tried to rescue one of the Israelites who were fighting with an Egyptian. The Egyptian was killed, and when Moses found out that other people knew about it, he fled to another country and became a shepherd there.

Moses was following the flock in the pasture. Suddenly, he saw a vision of a bush burning on the mountainside. Although it kept on burning, it was not consumed.

As Moses approached the burning bush, "The Angel of the LORD appeared to him in a flame of fire from the midst of a bush. So he looked, and behold, the bush was burning with fire, but the bush [was] not consumed. Then Moses said, 'I will now turn aside and see this great sight, why the bush does not burn.' So when the LORD saw that he turned aside to look, God called to him from the midst of the bush and said, 'Moses, Moses!' And he said, 'Here I am.' Then He said, 'Do not draw near this place. Take your sandals off your feet, for the place where you stand [is] holy ground. … Come now, therefore, and I will send you to Pharaoh so that you may bring My people, the children of Israel, out of Egypt.'... Then Moses said to God, 'Indeed, [when] I come to the children of Israel and say to them, "The God of your fathers has sent me to you," and they say to me, "What [is] His name?" what shall I say to them?' And God said to Moses, 'I AM WHO I AM.' And He said, 'Thus you shall say to the children of Israel, "I AM has sent me to you."'" (Exodus 3:1–14).

God sent Aaron to meet Moses, and together they headed toward Egypt. They gathered the elders of Israel and told them what the Lord had said. God assured Moses that He would be with Him, saying, "You shall go to all that I shall send you, and whatsoever I command you. Be not afraid of their faces for I am with you to deliver you says the Lord" (Jeremiah 1:7–8).

Moses and his brother, Aaron, went to Pharaoh and told him what God had said concerning His people, the Israelis. Pharaoh refused to let them go. God used all kinds of miracles and plagues until, at last, Pharaoh allowed the people of Israel to go to the Promised Land.

It's true that the gifts of God and His calling are not irrevocable. My ministry calling is very different. God called me into the ministry in 1985. He showed me a soul-thrilling vision, and I heard a voice saying, "Go! Reach the unreached with the gospel of love and hope." I know that my vision is twofold. Firstly, I was called to reach the unreached, and secondly, to give hope to the hopeless in this hurting world.

Serving the needs of people has not been as easy as some people may think. The most difficult call in my life has been to go out and meet other people's needs. The hardest ministry is working with people who are hopeless and have nothing to give you in return. Many ministers of the gospel want to work in towns or in cities where their congregation will provide them with large sums of money. Who then is called for needy? Tell some ministers about any needy person, and they will tell you, "I have no time for that issue, and I am not called in that ministry."

Ten needy cases will give the minister of the gospel sleepless nights. Is she or he really called by God? Jesus encouraged the needy by telling them, "I have compassion."

I don't want to blame ministers of the gospel, because I know they have different personalities and have adopted different characters from where they were brought up spiritually. Some came from different backgrounds than mine, others are not broken for ministry, and others have no ministerial mentorship. Ministers of the gospel are spiritually different. Some have some traditional barriers and understand the needy differently.

I have been given my vision, and I will not follow other people's visions. I have said that "I will obey my vision until the end." Some ministers of the gospel want me to follow their visions, but I will not. I will fulfill and focus on my vision; though it tarries what God will bring to pass. I was not called to please anyone but God.

I know my vision and my calling. I know the source of my calling. I will use my ministerial gifts, spiritual gifts, and motivational gifts to fulfill that vision.

All the trials and temptations I have experienced in the ministry to the needy are stepping stones into a greater ministry. I love my work and pray for those who oppose me, for I know they will steer me into my destiny. I will trust God to meet my needs and let Him defend me in the ministry. I will have faith in Him, for I know that without faith, it is impossible to please Him.

In my vision, God clearly showed me the map of Africa, which was shaped like a question mark. I saw millions of black faces of sinners, the needy, and the hurting people from many nations of Africa. When we look around our communities in Africa, what do we see? There are so many refugees, the homeless, the hopeless, the poor, the hungry, and the sick. HIV/AIDS and war are among the most common immerging issues in the nations.

In today's fast-paced society, we are always searching for new ways to handle stress in the lives of orphans, widows, HIV/AIDS victims, refugees, and the hurting. The key to handling the everyday stress in our lives is by having the inner peace, which is found in Jesus Christ only. The Bible calls Him a "wonderful counselor, mighty God, Everlasting Father, Prince of Peace" (Isaiah 9:6).

The only way to handle stress is by receiving Jesus Christ as your Savior. He is the prince of peace. The Bible says, "The poor are despised even by their neighbors, while the rich have many 'friends'" (Proverbs 14:20). The poor in our communities experience many problems; poverty exposes many to many temptations, dangers, sufferings, rejections, sicknesses, and other problems.

They try many things to survive with their families, but sometimes, they don't succeed. They pass through mental torture, emotional stress, failures, or embarrassment, and sometimes they go to bed hungry.

We are encouraging them not to lose hope. We are helping some to get a home or small business and solve domestic disputes. Their children suffer from abuse, not knowing what to do when they have problems such as sexual harassment, physical torture, mental torture, emotional torture, shame, guilt, fear, rejection, and neglect. They find solutions through God and our counseling sessions We are rescuing children from drug abuse before is too late.

CHAPTER FIVE

DELIVERED FROM DRUG ABUSE

KIM, NELLY, AND I WERE dancing champions in the disco halls of Nakuru Town. And my family and relatives only scorned me for the pleasurable life I was living there. My creditors marked me off as a bad debtor. My old pals avoided me like a dreaded disease. Then the time came when liquor no longer eased my quaking body nor calmed my enslaved mind. I was a complete wreck and a social misfit.

Despite this, my dear family planned to protect me by taking me out of the town to the Kiambogo farm and placing me in custodial care as a mental case. The fear of being committed to a mental institution became an obsession for me, and I completely yielded to their plans because I believed they would protect me.

I was given a plot, where I was expected to clear bushes and run a farming business. With the help of a panga, jembe, and axe, I became a charcoal burner, but one who hated and cursed his life. I was finally confined and put out of contact with decent society. My entire life and education were fully focused on rural development.

After several years on the farm, I became a devoted rural farmer in my home area. I was gradually impressed by the farming business, which brought great happiness in my life. Just try to imagine planting only a few seeds and awaiting what will turn out to be a great harvest and within a short time. I thank my dear family for their thought to rescue me.

Let me say that farming, despite being a good business, puts very many youths off. I was happy with my farming business, especially when I started earning some money, and with it, learning to be satisfied. My parents had tried to rescue me from the sinful life I was living in town by taking me to the Kiambogo farm in Elementaita. But in the terrible boredom of the up-country life, I was thinking about Nelly.

Nelly was a wonderful town girl. She was young and smart and calm by nature. She was always happy and friendly. To me, Nelly was a beautiful queen. She was my girlfriend. We used to walk together in town boldly. I could have never imagined that one day her name would sound so terrible to my ears.

In the up-country, life was very boring, and memories of Nelly were what kept me going. However, I had failed Nelly terribly. We were both lost in sin living that pleasurable life in town, but I knew that I had set her on a bad path. I was jobless and not ready to meet her needs as a husband. I did not own anything. I thought I would marry Nelly and settle down to discover what love is truly all about, but I only defiled and left her to bear the shame alone.

As I thought about my life and how I had messed up Nelly's life, I felt as guilty as a murderer. I was stricken with grief, and despair was written all over my face. This realization made me want to end my life. Several chaps of my age had done it before, one incident involving my friend.

I thought it was foolish for one to commit suicide, but what happened to me was just as my father had warned me about once: "Young man, there will come a time when all of your friends will deny you and the world will use you then fail you. You will wish you had listened to me. My son, I beg you to reform and come to realize the helpless predicament you are in before I die." *Was the old man right?* I asked myself. "All of my intimate friends detested me; those I love turned against me. I became nothing but skin and bones" (Job 19:19, 20 NIV).

I was a bad boy. I was corrupt, cruel, and dishonest. I was a slave to evil powers. I was trapped by enticements of Satan and the passions of the body. I was overtaken by drug addiction and alcoholism. I was a disco dancer with many traces of permanent physical damage. I was engulfed in anguish and despair. "If only my anguish could be weighed and all my misery placed on the scale! It would surely outweigh the sand of the seas..." (Job 6:2–3 NIV).

A feeling of desperation and helplessness passed through me as I came to grips with my hopeless situation. I was a teenager of twenty-three years who had nowhere to turn to for help. One day, my elder brother, David Muya, who at one time was worse off than me, came to me in the garden. He was holding in his hand a Bible, and when he gave it to me, my heart skipped a beat. The first words I read made me want to read more of the Bible: "FEAR NOT, ONLY BELIEVE" (Mark 5:36).

David told me to read the Bible and further persuaded me to change my sinful ways of life and receive Jesus Christ as my Savior. He assured me that God loves me. David then left me to read the Bible on my own. As I perused the pages, past memories of my livelihood shone vividly in my mind. I remembered my religious background and realized I was lost. A great conviction took a hold of my stubborn heart. This made me reconsider my ways and ask for forgiveness as I decided to return to my God.

To be frank, I was fearful that the conviction would not last. Many times, I had made resolutions that faded with time. Little did I know I was to come out of uncertainty and doubts unto a faith that is absolute truth without a shadow of doubt. My soul now became focused on the love of God.

I got to remembering how I, with the company of other youths, used to flock to all corners of Nakuru Town in search of dangerous drinks. "Woe unto them whom are mighty to drink wine and men of strength to mingle a strong drink" (Isaiah 5:22).

I had remembered my former life when I was brought up in a very humble way of life. Through the efforts of my mother, I attained good education. My family had sacrificed much through hard times for my upkeep. It surely would have been very hard for us children to survive if it were not for our mother, who cared for our welfare, especially our school fees.

My mother made money by the hard and even risky means of brewing the illicit liquor, "chang'aa," at night while escaping the police dragnet. This outlawed business was the lifeline of our family's income. My brothers and sisters were willing participants in this bad illegal business and even other worse money-making ventures taken in the name of survival.

I was profoundly disturbed by the bad traditional ways and hardships in which I had been brought up. I could not help my family to come out of the bad habits, for I did not know any scriptural quotes of the Bible. For me to stop such a successfully run business that made us survive, I had to make the life of my family uncertain. I started to cry as I thought deeply about my poor family.

At home, a friend gave me a book by author Billy Graham that explained to me on how to be born again. The title was "WORLD AFLAME." As I read it slowly page by page, the Word of God became real to me; that Jesus was knocking at the door of my heart. "Behold. I stand at the door and knock" (Revelation 3:19).

The next morning, I rose earlier than usual and set myself to consider what Jesus could do to fix my sinful life. "Oh, Jesus!" I cried, but there was no answer. I began to feel the terrible weight of my sins. "I will complain in the bitterness of my soul" (Job 7:11 NIV).

Sitting on my bed, I thought, *Will I be able to define the story of Jesus briefly to Nelly?* My mind was helplessly puzzled by this dilemma, for I was resolving to forsake Nelly once and for all. "No!" I said out loud with consciousness. I was not willing to lose the pleasures of this world yet.

All of these evil thoughts crossed my mind. However, they soon became buried down by the story of Jesus, which was resting on the bottom of my soul. *How shall I attain this supernatural power that would help me to overcome the evil love I hold for Nelly?* I thought with a humble heart. *After all, it was disturbing me. What will she say once she knows of my newly found faith in Jesus?* "What I feared has come upon me; what I dreaded has happened to me. I have no peace or quietness; I have no rest but turmoil" (Job 3:25, 26 NIV).

I was all alone on making the final decision. I knew I was to be opposed by all men of my age group, but I was ready to live a new life without sin. "Have pity on me, my friends. Have pity, for the hand of God has struck me. Why do you pursue me as God does?" (Job 19:22 NIV).

I had not heard any message on the new life in Jesus before, but upon reading through the Bible, I learnt that to die unforgiving and unchanged would mean to eternally perish in Hell. I was assured that I had despised the laws of God. Never in life had this awful truth from the Bible been so plain to me.

I looked again at the captivating words of God: "Fear not. Only believe." I felt Jesus standing by the door of my heart waiting for me to welcome Him in. After much reflection from the Word, I promised God that as soon as my season of youthful amusements was past, I would devote myself to eternal pursuits. However, the words kept ringing in mind.

I felt forsaken by the world and God standing by me. At first, I had no love of God in my heart nor repentance; nor did I wish to forsake sin. I felt nothing but solemn gloom and despair. I was now in the mighty hands of my creator from whom I expected mercy. "Hide thy face from my sins and blot out all mine iniquities" (Psalms 51:9).

Reading through the Bible, I became more and more acquainted with the Lord, Jesus Christ, and believed that my sins would be forgiven. I became fully convinced of this, for I had no other hope for my wretched condition. I learnt from the gospel that it is a must for me to repent my sins and receive JESUS CHRIST as my personal savior. Despite this, however, I planned to ignore the call of Christ due to my preference for the pleasures of sin. It was my greatest burden to have to lay in faith before my Lord.

What a terrifying experience this is, I wondered. I was badly off financially. In my small hut, I had no stool or table; only a small lamp beside the bedrail. But because I was a bachelor, I did not worry too much about having no money and no expectation to receive any. But due to what were indeed hard times, I often felt worthless. I lay prostrate on my bed with my hands pressed over my ears to shut out the outside world of sin and concentrate on Jesus instead. I had a heart full of longings and compassion for this: that He paid everything for my sins, even the sins that I had committed in childhood.

People would not understand it, I thought, *but Jesus loves me.* Yes, I wanted this Jesus, but my distracted attention towards evil thoughts also disturbed and tortured me greatly. There was a great battle going on in my mind. Somewhere within me there was a voice that disputed this love of Jesus, but another voice told me that the time had come for a final decision; and Nelly had nothing to do with it. Definitely I had to lose Nelly and receive this universal lover—Jesus—or otherwise perish in Hell eternally.

That night, I went to bed as usual, but for this reason I could not sleep. I therefore decided quickly to receive Christ as my Savior. I thought of saying a little prayer, and sure enough, without wasting any time, I went down on my knees and prayed. Soon I felt the touch of God in my soul, and the battle in my mind went raging.

I did not know exactly what was happening, but I felt something very real and frightening that took place. I tried to move out of bed, but I could not. There was such a powerful free Spirit that was holding me tight. I felt very sorry for my sins, for I realized just how much of a mess I had made of myself. As I felt power in my soul, I cried to God in faith for help in a loud voice.

I cried, "Have mercy upon me! Oh, God, according to thy loving kindness, according unto the multitude of thy tender mercies, blot out my transgression. Wash me thoroughly from my iniquity and cleanse me from my sins, for I acknowledge my transgressions; and my sin is ever before me. Against thee and thee only have I sinned and done this evil in thy sight; that thou mightiest be justified when thou speaketh and clear when thou judges" (Psalms 51:1–4).

I thanked God for saving me. I found myself lying in bed helplessly, bathed in sweat. I had asked for the power of JESUS CHRIST. He came and caught me by my right arm, picked me up, and then wrapped His nailed hands around me. I felt fresh after the blood of Christ cleansed me everywhere in my senses and conscience. All this happened in the spirit and in my soul. God's power crushed every sin within me and all the evil in my heart was removed; I came to feel the Son of God, virgin born, in my soul. He died for me on the cross. I saw Him standing looking at me with eyes full of compassion and great grace. He gazed at me and then said to me personally, "Fear not. I am Jesus."

God's love burst into my heart like a timed bomb. I mourned bitterly for my life and rubbed my forehead with the bed covers to wipe the sweat pouring off me. "It's a fearful thing to fall into the hands of the living God" (Hebrews 10:31). Jesus came into my heart, and I heard His voice in my heart saying, "Fear not. I'm Jesus." Truly His very name is love in itself.

My heart was throbbing within me. I breathed heavily and was trembling in the presence of Holy God. If I had listened to the voices of the evil spirits, I could have killed myself and spent eternal life in hell.

"Have any pleasure at all that the wicked man should die?' saith the Lord God. 'Or that he should return from his ways and live?'" (Ezekiel 18:23). I will not let anybody tell me that there is no chance at salvation for a wicked man, for Jesus is life and strength. "Neither is there salvation in any other, for there is no other name under Heaven given among men; whereby we must be saved" (Acts 4:12).

I was somewhat relieved. I lifted up my head, not yet conscious of all that had happened. I did not know what to say, since there were some powers holding me tightly. I could no longer see anything or anybody, nor could I hear anything. I sat on my bed, my face wet with tears and my mouth full of saliva. I felt very weak, as if some of my muscles had been ripped from my body.

I could now consider the past; the untidy, unplanned past, and it made me feel pity and shame before my God. I could not cry anymore. I wiped my face like a child recognizing the power of his or her loving father. I thought again of my former life and discovered that I was a hard creature grown in sin and evil. I was like a victor from a battlefield who found an escape from a prolonged bombardment.

It was with much pleasure that I realized that Jesus loves me and was real to me. My heart was filled with joy and peace. I turned slowly to the side of my wooden bed, struck a match, and lit my lamp to find that there was nobody in sight. However, there was someone in my heart. He was real. I could sense that I was no longer alone. There was power and an unseen somebody in my heart; this I knew was certainly the presence of Jesus.

Instantly, after this experience, I sat back in bed with a tremendous awareness that I had just been saved from death unto life through the blood of Jesus Christ. I was made alive again, and I was also freed from the prince of this world. All of the spirits of demonic oppression were gone, and I was free from sin, passions of the flesh, and desires of the heart.

"By nature, I was a child of wrath, like the rest of mankind. And you hath He quickened; of whom were dead in trespasses and sins. Where in time past you walked according to the course of this world; according to the prince of the power of the air, the spirit that now worketh in the children of disobedience. Among whom also we all had our conversation with in times past in the lust of our flesh; fulfilling the desires of the flesh and of the mind. Whom were by nature the children of wrath, even as others. But God is rich in mercy, for His great love where with

He loved us, even when we were dead in sins, hath quickened us together with Christ. By grace, ye were saved, and hath raised us up together and put us together in heavenly places in Christ Jesus" (Ephesians 2:1-6).

CHAPTER SIX

I SURVIVED DEATH

AS A DRUG ADDICT, I was involved in many fist fights in the village. Sometimes I would be seen sleeping in one corner of the village during late hours of the night. I used to command a group of twelve addicts. Some of my friends would be caught by the police and spend the night in jail cells.

We experienced nasty tragedies in the village. Every day you could hear disappointing and miserable stories of injuries and crime. The police were frequent visitors.

The worst thing that happened in my life was when I was involved in a very tragic road accident on the Nairobi-Nakuru Highway near Mbaruk trading center. I did not know how it really happened because I was drunk, but when I regained consciousness in the middle of the night, I was bedridden in Ward Five at the Nakuru Provincial Hospital with very serious injuries.

I was riding towards home when I was suddenly hit by a speeding lorry. I was found and taken to the hospital by a good Samaritan. The lorry had disappeared from the scene and left me by the roadside. I was told how I was bleeding on the ground after the accident in a near-death condition.

I was taken to the operating theatre in the hospital, and the doctors corrected the fracture. I remained in a cast for two months. The doctors saved my life. I survived death by a whisker. Despite the event, I still continued to drink after I recovered. This near-death experience and how much pain it had brought me were forgotten. I forgot how my clothes were soaked in blood and how others thought I could not survive. But luckily, I had survived by God's grace.

This is why I am saying that there is death in the pot of the illicit brew. The devil's plan was to kill me before I repented my sins, but God's plan was to use me as His servant in this hurting world. Many families are crying foul after the death of their loved ones in the drinking dens. Their hearts are broken, and they are looking for preachers to encourage and comfort them.

I was living in economic turmoil, chaos, and agony on every side. In the hospital, I remained unconscious for many hours. My family visited me and was shocked to see my face covered in bandages and my hand covered with a cast. When I woke up after the accident, I was surprised to see myself surrounded by beautiful ladies and doctors in uniform. They were checking my condition.

I remembered early one morning when my mother and father visited me. They thanked God that I was alive. My mother started to spoon-feed me, and she was looking at one of my casts without saying a word, while my father was dumbfounded.

In the hospital, people visited me, and I thanked God that I had survived death. After the accident, my family members were told that I would not survive. Even the patients in the ward encouraged and comforted me.

My father was scolding me, saying, "Look at what you are going through because of involving yourself with alcohol and drugs." I wondered how even in the hospital bed my father could not actually say an encouraging word to me. A few minutes later, the nurses in the ward told my visitors that their time was over, so they waved goodbye to me and left me alone in the ward.

Every morning, and during lunch time, my mother visited me in the hospital. She continued with her visits until I was discharged.

At home she nursed me back to health; cooking for me until I recovered fully. But the bad thing was that when I recovered, I continued with my evil behaviors. I forgot about how much I had struggled in the hospital bed with so much pain in my body. Many people in our village welcomed me back with a drink, and the addicts welcomed me back with rolls of drugs for free.

My life was full of ups and downs. I could remember the story of my near-death experience; it reminded me that there was still a light at the end of the dark tunnel in my life. God had spared my life for a reason, though I was not aware of it at the time. When the patients told me that I had been involved in a road accident the previous day, I remember praying secretly and telling God that if He would heal me, I would become a different person. But regardless, I once again became hooked on drugs and alcohol.

I was involved in a road accident because I was drunk and reckless. My bad judgment on the road drifted me into the accident. I will never forget that traumatic day for the rest of my life.

I grew tired of living with all these evil behaviors. I wanted to return to God. I remembered that in my Sunday school days I was taught that there is a beautiful place in heaven reserved for those who live a holy life in this world. I wanted to live a holy life and be counted with the holy ones in the church. With every fiber of my being, I wanted to be saved, but I was overwhelmed by fear that it would not last. I remembered how God had allowed me to survive a car accident, but then I desperately needed God to save me from sin, bondage, and addictions. I was trying not to drink with my own will power, but I could not control the craving by myself.

I was plugged into drinking again; the addicts welcomed me back into their drinking circle with cheers and free drinks. They made sure that even when I wasn't there I wouldn't be sober. The wine sparkled in the glass, and I craved it. But after consuming the drink, it would bite me like a serpent and sting me like a viper. Drinking made me poor; clothed in rags and worn-out shoes. My family pitied me. My creditors marked me off as a bad debtor. My body was racked with alcohol-related complications.

Together with my brothers and sisters, we all suffered physically, emotionally, and mentally, and we carried these inner hurts and scars into our adulthood. By the time David and I became teenagers, we were drug addicts. We would both get involved in fist fights and assaults, which were inflicted on women and girls. We were taken to the police cells on several occasions because of our crimes. In one drinking spree, when my brother assaulted a group of gangsters, he was beaten by the group almost to death. When he was rushed to Nyahururu Hospital, the doctors saw that both of his legs were broken. He remained with casts on both of his legs for three months.

In our family, alcohol was responsible for more admissions to hospitals than any other single cause. My father, mother, brothers, and sisters were also each taken to police cells because of alcohol-related crimes in the village before. Alcohol caused my father's death. It caused injuries in our bodies, and it broke our lives and hearts. It fractured both our family and our bones. It caused misery, hopelessness, and agony in our family.

The illegal business of brewing, drinking, and selling illicit brew brought even more misunderstandings, misery, confusion, stress, frustration, violence, crime, and wickedness in our family. In a time when the village Christians visited our family to comfort and encourage us following the occurrence of one of the many tragedies and incidents that happened in our family, my elder brother David accepted Jesus Christ as his personal Savior. He was saved, delivered, and totally transformed. And one year later, after observing my brother's changed life, I also accepted Jesus Christ as my personal Savior. I was finally delivered from sins, bondage, and addictions. Suddenly, no more drugs, alcohol, or sexual immoralities.

David and I joined the Full-Gospel Church in Kiambogo. We grew spiritually in this local church. My brother became a teacher in a primary school, and I became a gospel preacher in the village church. I then later started my own ministry, "Gospel Messenger's Church."

Today, I am a bishop, and I am saving many people from living as slaves of sin, bondage, and addictions. My purpose is to rescue children, youth, and families who are suffering from evil habits and addictions. I am dealing with these harmful and habit-forming drugs and alcohol.

The Bible says that drunkards and murderers will not inherit the Kingdom of God (1 Corinthians 6:9-10). It further says, "At last, it bites like a serpent and stings like an adder" (Proverbs 23–32). Alcohol does indeed bite like a serpent and sting like an adder.

The best treatment is total abstinence from alcohol and drugs by accepting Jesus Christ as your savior. Jesus saved me and completely changed me from a drug addict into a witness of Jesus Christ. Although I was a young man, I became a powerful preacher in wining souls for Christ.

For a few years in the Kiambogo village, I was appointed as a full-time pastor in the full-gospel church. That's when I married Mary Gathoni, a Christian lady and teacher in the village school. I had fallen in love with her, and four years later we were married in the church. I started witnessing to my friends, relatives, and neighbors, and many people joined my church. In the year 1984, my father died of an alcohol-related disease known as "cirrhosis." Having lived through many trials, tragedies, and disappointments in life, I started ministering hope, love, and faith to the hurting people in the village.

My campaign was against the harmful effects of drug abuse and alcoholism, which was dubbed "I shall not die but live and declare the works of the Lord" (Psalms 118:17). "I shall not die." I used open-air meetings as well as Christian films, books, and leaflets to reach the youth in schools, villages, towns, and colleges. I have rescued many youths from drug abuse and alcoholism.

In the villages, I started preaching peace. I told villagers the story of Jesus as the prince of peace. What is peace? Peace is the absence of mental anxiety. It's a state of living in harmony and serenity. It is freedom from war and fighting. People in the village were slaves of the illicit brews, and you could hear about many cases of domestic violence, rape, and assault. That's why I preached peace and organized peace forums in the villages. I had a very comprehensive mechanism for resolving family disputes.

I gave victims of circumstances hope for survival. In the village they called me "The Peace Messenger," a nickname for my distinguished role in building peace within the community. I had an outstanding record of handling difficult issues related to both families' conflicts and community conflicts. The suffering of the people is deeply etched into my life. My vision is to reach the unreached and give hope to the hopeless and the hurting.

I know the Almighty in His throne in heaven is watching over the hurting in Africa. We are giving hope of survival to the needy, the homeless, the hungry, the poor, and the hurting. God's mighty hand is moving as never before; saving, healing, delivering, and changing the whole continent of Africa. As a messenger of peace, I do declare that there is "Hope for Survival."

Today, Jesus is alive in my soul. I spend a wonderful time of anticipation and excitement as I enjoy His peace, joy, and salvation at all times during my life. My joy is not found only during the season of Christmas; the joy of my salvation flows in my soul all the days of my life. I can boldly say that I have experienced salvation with its fullness of inner peace and inner joy. That's why I'm going out in the marketplaces, streets, villages, towns, schools, and colleges encouraging people to accept Jesus Christ as their personal savior as well. I am approaching the government, counties, and NGOs to support me in my campaign against drug abuse and alcoholism dubbed "I Shall Not Die."

This problem is beyond legal approach alone. It is a social problem that needs heaven's intervention. As a minister of the gospel, I am fighting against drug abuse and the consumption of illicit brews. This fight should not be left entirely up to the government and other stakeholders; the church should be totally involved. This joint venture should be handled through teamwork and partnership with all stakeholders. That's why, on my part, I am totally involved.

I am strengthening my outreach capacity to effectively campaign against this vice that is threatening our youth. The menace of drug abuse is preying on our youth, on whom the future leadership and the economy is dependent, particularly in our aspiration of achieving our vision for 2030.

Drug abuse is a serious security challenge. "I shall not die" but I will live to preach the gospel in this hurting world. My redeemer lives. God called upon me to preach the gospel to orphans, disowned children, widows, drug addicts, and the hopeless. My father died from an alcohol-related disease, my sister followed in the year 2000 of HIV/AIDS, and my brother followed in the year 2003 from the same pandemic. In the year 2005 my mother died as a Christian.

After my father died, I started an outreach program to rescue drug addicts from abuse. I live by my faith in Christ in my life, family, and ministry. It's by God's grace, and by resilience, that I am able to focus on reaching the unreached. My focus is outward; I think more about the hurting and not just about me and my family. I don't allow anything to break my heart to the point in which I'd become bitter and give up in my ministry to reach the hurting. I am not broken down, but I am built up so that I can be all that God has intended for me to be. This all demands great spiritual resilience from my family and ministry. God has taught us how to endure during hard times. It is not the size of the soldier in the fight but the size of the fight in the soldier that matters. And God has prepared my spirit to be resilient for this fight.

One wise man said, "The strongest oak of the forest is not the one that is protected from the storm and hidden from the sun. It's the one that stands in the open where it is compelled to struggle for its existence against the winds, rain, and scorching sun." That's why in my ministry to the needy and hurting, I can sing popular Christian hymns to commemorate the death of my father. "When peace like a river attends my way, or when sorrows like the sea billows roll, whatever my lot, you have taught me to say, 'It is well, and it is well with my soul.'"

Psychologists say that resilience is not an extraordinary human trait that just a few people have, but I had to embrace it. The death of my father that happened because of his consumption of too much chang'aa brought a flood of strong emotions to me as a believer. I started an outreach program believing that there shall be no more deaths from illicit brews. God has helped me to rescue thousands of both old and young people from their evil behaviors and addictions.

Former drug addicts are helped to adapt to life-changing situations. They have received Jesus Christ as their personal Savior, and they are strengthened to overcome all manners of sins and bondage in their lives. I help them to walk again by faith after they fall. I have helped many to recover from addiction-related diseases.

I have resilience in my ministry to the needy and the hopeless. Resilience is an ongoing process that requires time and effort. It involves teaching about behaviors, thoughts, and actions that anyone can learn and develop, including setting realistic goals and working towards achieving them.

I'm working closely with a caring and supportive family and group of a few church members. It's necessary to constantly encourage myself in this tough ministry. I don't blame or beat up myself for setbacks. I remain confident that God, who gave me this ministry, will back it to the end. That's why I always like to be confident in His power and grace in my life and ministry.

I like helping others solve their problems and encouraging them in their mourning's. I don't harbor negative feelings but rather build on the positive. Quitting will never be an option for me, no matter what. I will never sit back, sigh, and wish things would change. I will never allow life's circumstances to push me down and hold me under again.

In my life and ministry, I have learned to take things easy. I believe the overwhelming blessings of God will continue to make me stronger in the Lord. Every year gives me an opportunity to make successes in scenarios where I thought I had failed. I was flipping years a few days ago and wondering just how resilient my family is. We are going to seize the future, shake off the self-limiting assumption that we are victims of circumstances, and resolve to live more graciously in Jesus Christ.

CHAPTER SEVEN

I WAS TRANSFORMED

IN 1978, I RECEIVED Jesus Christ as my personal Savior in the Kiambogo village in Elementaita. At the age of twenty-five years, in the year 1980, the Holy Spirit inspired me to write my first book entitled The Gospel Messenger. My aggressiveness in preaching the Gospel made the villagers nickname me, "The Gospel Messenger," a name that marched my virtue.

In the year 1985, God visited me in a soul-thrilling vision at night. I saw the Almighty Lord sitting on His throne in heaven. Before me laid a picture of the map of Africa, which was shaped like a question mark. Within the map, I saw millions of black faces of sinners and needy, poor, and hurting people from different nations of Africa. Many of these desperate people looked very helpless, hopeless, sick, hungry, homeless, and hurting. Some of them were crying and weeping helplessly.

I saw God changing the whole continent of Africa with His great power. In my mind, I thought, "Africa belongs to God." As I looked at the map, transfixed, I was awestruck by God's mighty presence and glory. A voice spoke to me, "Go! Reach the unreached with the gospel of love, peace, and hope!" And suddenly, I woke up with a vivid memory of this awesome vision from heaven. It was a clear confirmation that God had called upon me to be a gospel messenger.

Since then, my mission has been "Woe unto me if I don't preach the Gospel" (1 Corinthians 9:16). My vision was to reach the unreached and give hope to the hopeless in this hurting world.

I said, like the apostle, Paul, that "I was not disobedient to the heavenly vision" (Acts 26:19). This vision made me remember the prophetic message delivered by the famous world evangelist, Dr. T.L. Osborn, who was speaking in a soul-winner's seminar in Nakuru, Kenya, in the year 1979. He said, "Africa belongs to God! God is going to send Africans in different parts of the world to preach the Gospel, and especially in the continent of Asia."

God confirmed the same message in the year 1999 when the famous world prophet, Dr. Morris Cerullo, came to Nairobi for a world conference. He said, "God is going to raise up Africans. They will not only be used to reach Africans but the whole world." He concluded his message with powerful prayers for Africa. As he prayed, ministers of the Gospel in Africa were slain in the Holy Spirit, praising and worshiping God with tongues on the floor. The presence of God came down as never before.

In the year 2000, I registered my ministry in Kenya: "Gospel Messenger's Church." I started opening churches in the nearby villages, towns, cities, and counties. As I preached the message of love, peace, and hope to the hurting, tears of joy flowed in the eyes of sinners as they came forward to receive Jesus Christ as their personal savior after the altar call. Recently, in Nakuru in the year 2014, Dr. Morris Cerullo said in a leader's conference that Africa will receive an incredible breakthrough.

My life of exemplary faith in the ministry can be credited to my brother, David, because he is the one who led me to Jesus Christ. Ever since that blessed day of my visitation in my life in a vision, Africa has been in my heart and the world in my mind. I encourage believers in their walk of faith. I have written five books on faith to encourage the hopeless in this hurting world. Likewise, I have written five books on hope. And I have written four books on the theme of love. I need prayers and moral support to make my vision and ministry a reality.

It has been more than forty years since I started preaching the message of holiness and repentance. I have preached the power of the cross and Jesus as the source of joy, peace, love, and all the things that people ever wanted in this life. In my ministry, I have experienced trials and tragedies, but God has brought me through all of them.

Sometimes I experienced problems in which the one thing I could trust and count on to overcome them was the promises of God in His world. I do believe that "I am what God says I am. I can do what God says I can." Furthermore, I am God's property, for all my questions in life have been answered. This confident assurance enables me to remain calm through all circumstances of life. I have stability in Jesus Christ and an inner foundation that holds me up whenever life threatens to overwhelm me. I keep swinging at life's tough trials as I serve my God in all circumstances in this hurting world.

Today, I am busy reaching the unreached and giving hope to the hopeless on this continent of Africa. I'm a gospel messenger. I'm working as a herald who is expecting to see the greatest outpouring of the Holy Spirit in Africa. That is why my message is "Repent, Africa." My message is simple. "Repent and be converted so that your sins may be blotted out and a time of refreshing may come from the presence of the Lord" (Acts 3:19). Africa is in my heart and the world in my mind. This vision sounds like an impossible thing to fulfill, but I'm used to seeing God accomplish the impossible things, for with God, nothing will be impossible (Luke 1:37).

My hope is in God. "Now faith is the substance of the things not seen but hoped for." (Hebrews 11:1) The evidence of hope is a very powerful means of strengthening me in prayer. I pray with great hope that God will hear my prayer. My hope is fixed upon God's world. Hope is the anchor of my faith that God is faithful to fulfill this promise and that He will never alter the things He has spoken with His mouth. I am diligent in prayer; therefore, I will never be destitute of hope. "Whatever things were written sometime were written for learning that through patience and comfort the scriptures might have hope" (Romans 15:4).

There is no time when I will stop hoping because my hope is founded on God. Hope is stronger than wishing and more active than longing. Hope desires with an earnest expectation of fulfillment. "But as for me, I will hope continually—and I will praise thee yet more and more" (Psalms 71:14). I hope that for the second coming of Jesus Christ, He remains my constant inspiration. This hope is cheering me during lonely hours and moving me to fresh efforts to preach the gospel as never before.

Recently, the world leaders held a global peace forum in Geneva, Switzerland. The main agenda of this forum was peace and security. All world leaders tried to tackle various challenges facing the world today. Among the various global security challenges was terrorism, which stood out as one of the most sophisticated and challenging to handle. Terrorism is a human-imposed disaster aimed at maximizing mass destruction through the use of violent action in order to achieve a political agenda. Everywhere in the world, we are hearing cries for peace in nations' cities, towns, villages, schools, colleges, and homes. World leaders are making strategies that can be used nationally and internationally only to end up as terrorism.

Terrorists target crowds of people, infrastructure, and other strategic installations that are very crucial to the survival of states or nations. Through mass destruction, terrorists are killing many innocent people, and they are destroying properties worth billions of dollars. They target some specific nations or states.

Terrorism, with all its manifestations and activities, violates human rights of people. Terrorism is one of the prophetic signs of the second coming of Jesus Christ. World leaders are fighting this threading monster. By working with an intelligence report, security is being maintained in the nations around the world. In our country, these attacks of terror are damaging our nation's reputation and peace. The consequences of these terrorist attacks have further resulted in reduction of tourism flow to our country as well as investment flow.

All these threats of mass destruction and rumors of war are experienced in many nations of the world. That's why, as a prophet to the nations, I'm thanking God, for He has protected and preserved us. Many people in this world have forgotten God, like Sodom and Gomorrah. Our loving God has given the world a clear way of escaping the coming judgment. The way is receiving Jesus Christ, who is the Savior, Redeemer, and Prince of Peace in this world.

Jesus is the answer to you, your nation, and the whole world. We need God in Africa. Although Africa is shaped like a question mark, we have answers in Jesus Christ. God loves Africa, and that is why we cry, "Africa for Jesus!" Let's repent our sins now and live in holiness in order to escape the coming judgment from God. The day of our salvation is now.

• • • •

CHAPTER EIGHT

MY MISSION

THROUGHOUT MY CHRISTIAN life, there have been trials, temptations, and tragedies, but I thank God, for He had guided me through all of them. The infilling of the Holy Spirit that I had received made me to be strong in the Lord. The Holy Spirit has helped me to grow up spiritually and continues to move on from glory to glory. Where the Spirit is, there is power and liberty. I have confident assurance of having God's protection in my life, which has enabled me to remain calm through all the circumstances that life throws at me. I thank God that Jesus has promised to be with me throughout my whole life.

That's why I represent Him here on Earth. There is no greater honor on Earth than that of working with Jesus as His ambassador. The spirit of God creates a passion in my heart that Satan cannot extinguish. In spite of severe occurrences of testing, failures, and discouragements, I have never had another passion in my life as strong as that of serving God under the Spirit's anointing.

There is no greater joy and satisfaction than that of being used by God in any capacity whatsoever. I'm always more than willing to speak about God in any place or circumstance. In my life, preaching is very important. I'm glad that I keep my eyes firmly fixed on the source of power—Jesus Christ.

Romans 8:31–35 says, "What shall we then say to these things? If God be for us, who can be against us? He who spared not his own son but delivered Him up for us all? How shall He not with Him also freely give us all things? Who shall lay anything to the charge of God's elect? It is God that justifies. Who is he who condemneth? It is Christ who died, yea rather, who had risen again; who is even at the right hand of God, who also maketh intercession for us. Who shall separate us from the love of Christ? Shall tribulation, or distress, or persecution, or famine, or nakedness, or peril, or sword?"

There is one source of inspiration from which in particular I derived a fire in my belly, which made it possible for me to be a power-packed gospel messenger. I first received guidance from the teachings of Rev. T.L. Osborn and his wife in a soul-winner's seminar in Nakuru Town. He had a big crusade and later taught in a seminar in a big tent. His words were much anointed; to which I will remember them as long as I live, and I hope you will also. He said, "I am an ambassador of Christ. I am more than extraordinary; I am what God says I am. I can do what God says I can."

After the seminar, these words were still ringing in my heart, and T.L. Osborn kept teaching me through the mail. He also sent me a supply of soul-winning and faith-building books and sermon tapes and tracts. As I read the books and listened to the tapes, the zeal of God began to consume me. It kept burning in my soul. There was a driving force in my spirit; a fire that couldn't be quenched. My soul was moved by great love for the lost world. It was time for me as an ambassador of Christ to stop floundering around being generally preoccupied with my own agenda and problems and instead move on in faith to make a difference in this hurting world.

I am glad to say that the efforts made by T.L. Osborn and his wife to teach and encourage me were not in vain. His teachings have changed the whole of Africa. Today, "Africa is for Jesus." We have now a powerful gospel mission of reaching the rest of Africa with the gospel of love. And in my life, I have been telling God to take me into an unprecedented manifestation of his word through the teachings of Morris Cerullo, which boldness me to continue with my vision.

I have another inspiration from R.W. Schambach, who is both my friend and my critic. I thank God for the prayers of these men of God and the power they have imparted in my life and ministry. Through their powerful and life-changing teachings, they have revived me to touch many more lives. It is my prayer that God will continually bless their ministries and families.

I depended entirely upon God for daily spiritual upkeep. And so, I became a young power-packed gospel messenger; a very effective soul-winner. I was also very pleased to work hand in hand with various gospel ministry organizations around the world. My burden is to obey God's command, which is to preach the gospel to every creature on Earth. My vision is "Reaching Africa for Jesus."

For many years in this fruitful ministry, I have come to know the answers to the many questions that had long troubled me before I got saved. I will bless the Holy Spirit for coming into my new heart. I will bless the day I was born again. I will bless my ministry. I will bless the angels for becoming faithful guardians in my life. I will thank the Lord very much for blessing me in a wonderful way. "Oh, what a great change—out of being a hopeless charcoal burner into a power-packed gospel messenger." Praise the Lord.

After waiting upon the Lord, I'm glad to let you know that I was blessed with a beautiful lady who is my wife today. We are also blessed with two daughters and a son. "He who finds a wife finds a good thing and obtains favor from the LORD" (Proverbs 18:22). "Your wife will be like a fruitful vine within your house, and your children will be like olive shoots around your table" (Psalms 128:3).

I am not proud about my past, but I must speak plainly to everybody about this wonderful experience that brought an inward peace and love from God, which has been an anchor of the glorious hope of Jesus in me. I have a consuming desire to preach the gospel, and I am deeply convinced that God had called me to the ministry. I'm a full-time pastor who has surrendered his life to his ministry.

By the love of God in my life, I have discovered the answer to the main question that had long troubled me: Why was I born? I was born to preach the gospel; to reach Africa for Jesus. Praise the Lord! "Where there is no vision, the people perish" (Proverbs 29:18).

As I use my special abilities in God's work, He is quick to respond, confirming His promises with miracles and wonders. To me, it is great to serve this wonderful God. I truly consider it a great privilege to be His ambassador and let Him reach others through me in Africa.

Has He not filled me with the Holy Spirit and told me personally, "Fear not; I am Jesus"? Yes, He has! And I will serve and love Him with all my strength. Jesus is my closest friend. "You are my friends if you do whatever I command of you" (John 15:14). I do not always understand how God performs miracles, but I rejoice whenever His love brings about transformation of souls and bodies. I very much appreciate and love our ministry because through it and other ministries I am brought up spiritually.

I like writing tracts because of how wonderful they are. I write testimonies of what the Lord is doing in my life today. God has opened doors for me. And I know that many of my tracts are preaching to thousands, and possibly to millions, in this country and overseas. I have had requests from many lands with reports of blessings.

This is a ministry that requires steadfast faith, for when you write a tract, few people write back in thanks for a tract that had blessed them. I thank God that He has encouraged me to write. "He who winneth souls is wise" (Proverbs 11:30).

Jesus is my hope. "Now the God of Hope fills you with all joy and peace in believing that ye may abound in hope; through the power of the Holy Ghost" (Romans 15:13). Thank you, Jesus, for being my closest friend. My hope is built on nothing else but Christ. I dare not trust in any false hope but lean on Jesus, the solid rock of all ages.

Question: Have you made this commitment of faith to Jesus Christ? God is always calling people into His kingdom: "Come unto me all ye who labour or are heavy laden and I will give you rest" (Matthew 11:28). Jesus will deliver you from all such things, like riots, evil demonstrations, threats, murder, suicide, sex-perversion, drug addiction, jealousy, pride, diseases, and alcoholism. The Bible says: "He who covereth his sins shall not prosper, but whoever confesseth and forsaketh them shall have mercy" (Proverbs 28:13).

The world today is in the hands of a demon-inspired youth who seem to drag it down to degradation and damnation. That is the reason why the Bible says: "Rejoice, O' young man, in thy youth, and let their hearts cheer thee in the days of thy youth and the sight of thine eyes; but know thou, that for all these things God will bring thee into judgment" (Ecclesiastes 11:9).

My dear friend, respond to God's calling right now, for He is standing at the door of your heart now waiting for you to open it for Him. Will you? Why would you be afraid to say before your Lord and creator, "I'M SORRY, LORD"? For sure you will experience another moving power that will cause you to say, "THANK YOU, LORD!" Jesus will conquer all your negative thoughts and make you a completely new person, as you would like to be. His name is love! "But God commendeth His love towards us in that while we are still sinners; Christ died for us!" (Romans 5:8).

My friend, God loves you very much, and so do I. It is my prayer that God's love through Jesus Christ will be manifested in your life, and therefore, you will become a completely new person, as God desires that for us.

For more help, write soon, for I am always ready and prepared to take the Gospel anywhere. My prayer is, "Lord, make the nations my heritage and the ends of the Earth my possession" (Psalms 2:8). Finally, after a long struggle, I have surrendered my life to the ministry. I am glad that the Lord meets all my financial needs. I will joyfully represent Him here on Earth and do His words. "Behold. I will send my messenger" (Mark 1:2).

My mission is to save children of God from the hands of wickedness, undo heavy burdens, let the oppressed go free, and break every yoke of the enemy (Isaiah 5:6). I distribute gospel tracts to schools, public places, hotels, bars, disco halls, universities, colleges, hospitals, cinema halls, and nightclubs. My motto is to "preach the gospel to every creature." We messengers of God are sent to preach the gospel to every creature in this world. Let your prayer be, "Lord, make me a gospel messenger for you." Believe in the Lord, your God, and you shall be established; believe His prophets, and you shall prosper" *(II Chronicles 20:20).*

Called To Win Souls for Christ

Yes! I was called to win souls for Christ
The silent kid which love assails
Walks daily in the valleys of love eternal
Where I feel love, winds rattling
And eternal rivers running fast in my heart

Lord! In me thy love impact in Africa
In amusing honor, all men could hear the cry
Called to win souls for Christ
Great happiness is found in me
While crying for the souls of men
I sang my praises in the open
My joys from Jesus Christ flowed
Eternal life is found in Him
The peace they seek is also in Him
In Africa the blessed kid stood still
When I'm weak I'm strong
When my strength and self fails
The LORD my Savior prevails
I will fast and pray
For the souls of men in Africa
Raised as modern prophet
With heavenly visions and goals
Called to win souls for Christ
Lord before thy cross I kneel
Fill my craving heart with love
And a deep burning flame for souls
With a mighty anointing; baptize me
Teach me thy great work of soul-winning
Let me be a soul-winner here on Earth
And go with thee in the entire world to win souls
Called to win souls for Christ

MISSION: "Woe to me if I do not preach the gospel" (1 Corinthians 9:16)

CHAPTER NINE

I SHALL NOT DIE

GOD PUT A BURDEN ON the founders Christ Ordained Kids to minister healing to the hurting drug addicts and alcoholics in our communities .. Directors agreed to go out in the villages to fight the illicit brew menace that is a threat to our youths. The devil's business is to snare the victims with his chains; hands and feet. Our business is to go out and rescue our young people from the destructive addictions in Jesus' name!

In our organization, we know that before us there is a battle to be waged. This is the eleventh hour, and we are to move urgently if we are to rescue our brothers and sisters from the king down in darkness before it's too late! Our staff members are men and women who feel that they have been called by God to their brothers and sisters from life's greatest disasters. They are always ready to go out and put their lives at risk in order to transform drug addicts

The chairman, is Dr Kwake, in biblical studies and Christian counseling. The secretary Rev Jorom. He teaches former addicts entrepreneur skills in seminar A Member, Mr Ben, is a graduate who helps in preparing all of the teaching materials, including charts, posters, books, receipt books, flyers, and adverts on social media. He is also an ICT expert with a school for the same.

In our organization, we agreed that we shall be calling experts like Professor Susan Gitau, a psychologist, to come to our seminars to talk about the effects of drug abuse. Dr. Kassinga Kwake, Ph.D., lectures on life skills. And Rev. Joram, a business consultant, talks about entrepreneur skills in our seminars. We shall also be inviting our partners, the Equity Bank experts, to come to our seminars to talk about financial management to the former addicts so that they can start income-generating projects. We help former addicts start their livelihoods.

The team of our staff has stepped forward to fill the present gap by responding to the cries of the hurting drug addicts and alcoholics. Our team is ready to go to the slums, ghettos, and villages to give hope to the hopeless. They are willing to pay whatever price the Lord wants them to pay in order to rescue their brothers and sisters from destructive behaviors.

Do you have any information concerning the whereabouts of drug addicts and alcoholics? If so, please, contact us. We are an outreach organization, and our main objectives are well spelled out in this book. Read through it all, and together we shall make great strides.

Is survival possible? Where shall we get answers to the questions in our lives in Africa? Whether we admit it or not, deep in our souls we are hurting. We have a craving, a thirst for meaning in our lives. Trying alcohol and drug abuse leads us only to more troubles, such as ending up in jails for drug-related crimes. Conflict and civil wars lead us to the loss of our loved ones. We are living in a thirsty society with nothing to satisfy our craving for meaning.

This is why Bishop Muya, together with his team, registered "Stay Up Rehabilitation Community-Based Organization" to answer the questions that are being asked by drug addicts, alcoholics, and other hurting souls. They strongly believe that with God, survival is possible. Bishop Muya is giving hope for survival by inviting victims to drink from the wells of salvation. "Therefore, with joy shall we draw water from the wells of salvation" (Psalms 12:3). Victims should joyfully drink from the wells of salvation so that they shall get deliverance, peace, healing, success, prosperity, etc. If you are thirsty, God can fill your craving forever. Africa will not die but live. Africa belongs to God. With God, survival is possible in this hurting world!

Because many people in the villages of the Elementaita division are very much affected by drug abuse and alcoholism, this community-based organization is campaigning against this throat-burning menace in these villages. Addiction to substances is causing domestic violence in families, misuse of finances, chaos, crises, grief, loss, and even death. But through biblical teachings, this team is leading victims to healing, recovery, and wholeness after encouraging them to accept Jesus Christ as their savior. We are counseling with psychotherapy that is Christ-centered.

Bishop Muya is teaching victims entrepreneur skills after they recover from addiction. He also teaches the wives of the victims how to accept their husbands back home. He teaches practical advice and spiritual insights from a Christian perspective. He also encourages wives who have lost their husbands from drug abuse and alcoholism. He gives timeless wisdom to victims of rape, shock, emotional trauma, depression, and domestic violence. He leads them to compassionate and reassuring answers. He talks to them about resolving personal problems and meeting emotional needs right at their fingertips. He helps to solve problems of anxiety. Also marriage, and much more.

Bishop Muya has a unique resource for personal devotion as well as counseling. He has a healing resource with pastoral counseling. His recent research is qualifying him to give victims professional guidance in their situations or circumstances drawing from concrete passages. He gives victims hope for survival. He builds the victims' lives according to the plans drawn by the architect, God.

Bishop Muya's organization is following the blueprint from heaven. He has a team of facilitation who works in the organization.

From our organization, the position you should focus on beyond your own interest is the interests of the community. Our objectives were opened to serve the community. This is really good, but some of our team members were focusing on what they would get after serving the community. We are to focus on serving the community and not on what we would get from them. "The chairman briefed the meeting before the outreach team. No single member should be the center of attraction, and nobody should diminish the organization's ability to minister love and hope to the hurting community." That is what the chairman affirmed.

We are called to minister to the drug addicts and alcoholics. We should change and transform them completely. After a briefing, some team members said that they had come to truly understood the objectives of the organization. Everybody learnt that he or she should be fitting in the service to the community. Some team members apologized after having realized they were wrong. Their willingness to serve the hurting had not been evident. The morning after that briefing, some team members started serving the community even before having their breakfast. The chairman kept them updated through mobile phones.

When a fire broke out in the village where they were ministering, the chairman called members to donate money, food, and clothes to the victims. He asked them not to put value on material blessings, but rather give to get true happiness that can only be found in a relationship with Jesus Christ. Jesus gave his life for us, so let's give ourselves to the lives of the hurting.

You can be a volunteer for two weeks in our short-term mission to the community. We can fix you where you will fit in our outreach project to minister to the vulnerable kids, drug addicts, or elderly folks. We have volunteers; as in people who come out from their comfort zones to contribute to our successful outreach programs to the community. Our mission has improved the quality of services to the hurting lives.

If you want to experience God's blessings, volunteer to serve the community through our organization. One of our team members is doing a mobile job in ministering to the elderly who are having emotional problems in their lives. Many are suffering from abandonment and loneliness, which is hurting them the most.

Ann has helped several elderly folks who have succumbed to poor health; and some even could not walk to attend Sunday services. Ann prayed with them and read them some Scriptures before leaving them. The Holy Spirit has been working in Ann's life as she continues with her visitation and outreach programs. The empowerment of the Holy Spirit has been touching even the team members to join in the ministry to the elderly. This is a very important ministry in the community.

We are encouraging our outreach team to work with Ann help shine up the community. Let's show God's love in action to the needy and let's give them Jesus. Let's go out to relieve the pain of all those who are suffering from different problems in the villages. I remember a time in our outreach program when we met a drug addict in his house who said he had used drugs for many days but that when we told him about Jesus Christ and how He came to help the sinners and drug addicts, he surrendered his miserable life to Jesus Christ. This man was completely set free from addiction. And when he was testifying in our seminar, another drug addict surrendered his hopeless life to Jesus and transformed as well.

We are helping those with destructive behaviors and stress to recover. When the chairman called a meeting to encourage the former addicts, they joined the outreach team.

During the program, one team member reported about some students in two neighboring secondary schools who were caught abusing drugs by their teachers in the village over the holidays. So, we urgently conducted a community outreach program for the students in those two schools.

We noticed that when we approached the students in those schools, they were very willing to disclose their problems of addiction with drugs. After the program, some students were ready to quit from addiction and publicly surrendered their lives to Jesus Christ. They were totally delivered and transformed.

God has uniquely given each one of us a gift so that we can minister to the community. The chairman encouraged the students after the program to join the outreach team, and some of them did. They volunteered to help the team with details concerning drug addiction in schools. Together with them, we planned a very big outreach program for youths and students. And the youth and students were encouraged to see their friends in the outreach team.

Jane was one of the girl students who willingly joined the outreach team. She enjoyed the program when she was given a badge with the organization's logo. She carefully pinned it on her dress. Looking at herself in a small mirror, she smiled at how nicely the badge matched her dress. She admired it. "You look nice," the voice of Jane's friend, Mary, spoke. "Thank you, Mary," Jane responded in appreciation of her friend's comment.

Jane joined the other team members in a brief meeting before starting the program in the other school in the village. She learnt the importance of serving their community in love and what she should do to express her love to the hurting through actions. She had proved her commitment by volunteering to usher in the coming victims to be ministered to in the program.

In a drinking spree, a young lady was rescued by the village youth after a disagreement with a drug addict who was beating her. When she raised an alarm, the youths rushed to rescue her. One of our team members brought her into our office and she was ministered to. She is now among the praise team in the village church.

My name is Bishop Peter Njoroge Muya. I am a former drug addict from Nakuru County, Kenya. I have spent a lot of time fighting against the drug abuse and alcoholism that is rampant among the youth in my community.

The consumption of alcoholic beverages is as old as mankind. It began when the two Daughters of Lot made wine for their father and slept with him (Genesis 19, verses 30–38).

Dangers of alcohol consumption

THE CUSTOM OF CONSUMING alcohol has been tolerated among many African communities. Although legally accepted, alcohol has the potential to cause harm if abused. Traditionally, alcohol consumption was restricted to the elders. It provided a forum to exchange views, conclude community meetings, resolve disputes, formalize marriages, etc.

Alcohol consumption occupied a central role in communities' social activities. People drank for forms of celebration and not in a violent manner. Most of the African communities consumed fermented alcohol, which has less alcoholic content as opposed to the distilled alcoholic beverages.

But sadly, drinking alcohol has lost its traditional values. It has become commercialized. Teenage and student consumption has risen. The proliferation of adulterated and illicit brews has worsened.

While carrying out the mandate of creating a secure environment for social-economic development, alcohol and drug abuse has emerged as a major social challenge and threat to national security. In particular, it poses a serious threat to the productivity of the young people in the country.

Dangers of drug abuse

THE YOUTH TEND TO ENGAGE in crime as a way to sustain their drug-dependent lifestyle at the expense of engaging in productive endeavors. This worrying trend calls for a concerted effort to stem its upward growth because it is a major impediment of Kenya's vision.

The misuse, or abuse, of drugs in the country has resulted in serious socio-economic consequences. It's led to increases in: crime sprees, domestic violence, rape cases, divorces, poverty, and deaths.

A survey conducted by NACADA (National Campaigns Against Drug Abuse) a few years ago indicated that 13% of Kenyans between the ages of fifteen to forty years consume alcohol or abuse drugs. This survey had the most abused drug listed as the locally grown "bhang" and the most abused alcoholic beverage as the "second-generation brews." The end result is health complications and death. Because the tread of drug abuse is so worrying, a public program should be instituted as a matter of national priority from the villages to the county.

My campaign against drugs is dubbed as "I Shall Not Die." I have written a book to teach victims on the dangers of addiction entitled I Shall Not Die. My message in this book to the youth and the community is to embrace sobriety and avoid using drugs and avoid drinking this dangerous poison.

Join me in this campaign to end the menace that is addiction.

Outreach Project

-WE ARE USING OPEN AIR meetings, Christian films, Christian books, and other printed materials to reach the youths in the slums, villages, ghettos, schools, and colleges.

-I am working very closely with more than twelve facilitators. Mr. Daniel Kuto is one of the directors of this outreach program. Apart from teaching, he has a diploma in counseling, and he is training the community on how to avoid drug abuse.

-The objectives of the group are to teach people and the community on:

a) HIV/AIDS.

b) Hygiene and diseases prevention.

c) Drug abuse and alcoholism prevention.

We are working in collaboration with other facilitators, doctors, teachers, and spiritual leaders. We are trying to locate a big plot in which to build a rehabilitation center for drug abuse and alcoholism where victims can be exposed to entrepreneur ventures and be given solutions on many social

problems.

-We are encouraging addicts to start simple businesses to alleviate hopelessness, idleness, poverty, and crime.

-In our mission to the community, there are some factors that are hindering the spiritual and intellectual development. This includes:

1. Poverty
2. Unemployment
3. Illiteracy in many adults
4. Alcoholism and drug abuse
5. Cultural and traditional beliefs

The Gospel Messengers Church has been playing a virtual role through Bishop Muya in providing spiritual counseling. Especially to those who have been rehabilitated through this project.

To bring recognition to this vision and campaign, we are kindly requesting for good will from partners around the world, governmental organizations, and well-wishers to help us in capacity. We need resources in terms of funds to build rehabilitation centers, publish training materials, and buy electronic devices, e.g. laptops, tablets, and projectors. We'd also need a van for transporting facilitators to the outreach venues and for carrying equipment.

- Training and seminars

- Church activities

- Hall rent

- Stationary

- Transport and communication

- Field visit

- Monitoring and evaluation

- Learning resources

- Food

- Hygiene and sanitation

- Income-generating projects

- Loan mentorship

- Group vision creating awareness in disease management and reduction of drug abuse and alcoholism.

Mission

- To promote health management in the community.

Project Sustainability

- 1. Table banking
- 2. Loan mentorship
- 3. Community awareness on diseases
- 4. Drug abuse and alcoholism
- 5. Improving living standards of the rehabilitated people
- 6. Encouraging income-generating projects

We are willing to work together with all stakeholders we're targeting in this project. Help our outreach campaign against this destructive vice that is threatening our youth and the community. We are rescuing our youth from addiction because the economy is dependent on them. This is particularly our vision for 2030. We are asking the government and NGOs to support us financially.

CHAPTER TEN

COMMONLY ABUSED DRUGS AND THEIR TREATMENT

DRUG ABUSE AND ADDICTION is a complex but treatable disease that affects brain function and behavior, resulting in changes that persist long after drug use.

Treatment varies depending on the type of drug and characteristics of the patient, but some of the commonly abused drugs, of which are tabulated below, are treated with behavioral therapy.

Recovery from drug abuse and addiction is a long-term process, and it frequently requires self-realization on the part of the victim as well as their willingness to avoid returning to drug abuse. This is followed by multiple episodes of treatment. As with other chronic illnesses, relapses can occur and should signal a need for a treatment to be reinstated or adjusted.

Because individuals often leave treatment prematurely, programs should include strategies to engage and keep patients in treatment. The following are two examples of such strategies:

- Behavioral therapies
- Drug therapies

Behavioral Therapies.

Behavioral therapies, including individual, family, or group counseling, are the most commonly used forms of drug abuse treatment.

Behavioral therapies vary in their focus and may involve addressing a patient's motivation to change, providing incentives for abstinence, building skills to resist drug use, replacing drug-using activities with constructive and rewarding activities, improving problem-solving skills, and facilitating better interpersonal relationships.

Additionally, participation in group therapy and other peer-support programs during and following treatment can help maintain abstinence.

Drug Therapies

Drug therapies are an important element of treatment for many patients, especially when combined with counseling and other behavioral therapies.

For example, Methadone, Buprenorphine, and Naltrexone (including a new, long-acting formulation) are effective in helping individuals who are addicted to heroin or other opioids to stabilize their lives and reduce their illicit drug use. Acamprosate, Disulfiram, and Naltrexone are medications that are approved for treating alcohol dependence.

For people who are addicted to nicotine, nicotine replacement products (available as patches, chewing gums, lozenges, or nasal sprays) or oral medications (such as Bupropion or Varenicline) can be an effective component of treatment within a comprehensive behavioral treatment program.

Drug use during treatment must be monitored continuously, as lapses during treatment do occur. When the patients are aware that their drug use is being monitored, it can be a powerful incentive for them and can help them withstand urges to use drugs.

Treatment programs should also test for the presence of HIV/AIDS, Hepatitis B and C, Tuberculosis, and other infectious diseases, as well as provide targeted risk-reduction counseling, linking patients to treatment if necessary. Typically, drug abuse treatment addresses some of the drug-related behaviors that put people at risk of such infectious diseases. Targeted counseling focused on reducing infectious disease risk can help patients further reduce or avoid substance-related and other high-risk behaviors.

Counseling and behavioral therapy can also help those who are already infected to manage their illness. Moreover, engaging in substance abuse treatment can facilitate adherence to other medical treatments. The menace of drug abuse is preying on our youth on whom the future leadership and the economy is dependent, particularly in our aspiration of achieving our vision for 2030.

My father died from an alcohol-related disease. My sister followed in the year 2000 cervical cancer and my brother followed in the year 2003 from the same pneumonia. In the year 2005, my mother died as a Christian and I remembered how my father died, I started an outreach program to rescue drug addicts from abuse.

God called upon me to preach the gospel to orphans, widows, disowned children, drug addicts, and the hopeless. I live by my faith in Christ in my life, family, and ministry. It's by God's grace and by His resilience that I can focus on reaching the unreached. My focus is outward. I think more about the hurting and not just about my family and myself. I don't allow anything to break my heart to where I'd become bitter and give up in the ministry made to reach the hurting.

"I shall not die," but I will live to preach the gospel in this hurting world—my redeemer lives. I am not broken down, but I am built up so that I can be all that God has intended for me to be. It demands great spiritual resilience from my family and ministry. God has taught us how to endure during hard times. It is not the size of the soldier in the fight, but the size of the fight in the soldier that matters. God has prepared my spirit to be resilient for the battle.

One wise man said, "The strongest oak of the forest is not the one that is protected from the storm and hidden from the sun. It's the one that stands in the open where it is compelled to struggle for its existence against the winds, rain, and scorching sun." That's why in my ministry to the needy and hurting, I can sing popular Christian hymns to commemorate the death of my father. "When peace, like a river, attends my way, when sorrows like the sea billows roll, whatever my lot, you have taught me to say, 'It is well, and it is well with my soul.'"

Psychologists say that resilience is not an extraordinary human trait that just a few people have, but I had to embrace it. The death of my father, because of his consumption of much chang'aa, brought a flood of strong emotions to me as a believer. I started an outreach program in my belief so that I shall see no more deaths from illicit brews. God has helped me to rescue thousands of old and young people from evil behaviors and addictions.

Former drug addicts are helped to adapt to life-changing situations. They have received Jesus Christ as their personal Savior, and they are strengthened to overcome all manners of sins and bondage in their lives. I help them to walk again by faith after they fall. I have helped many to recover from addiction-related diseases.

I have resilience in the ministry to the needy and the hopeless. Resilience is an ongoing process that requires time and effort. It involves behaviors, thoughts, and actions that anyone can learn and develop, including setting realistic goals and working towards achieving them. I'm working closely with a caring and supportive family and a few church members.

It's necessary to continually encourage myself in this challenging ministry. I don't blame nor beat myself up for setbacks. I am confident that God, who gave me this ministry, will back it to the end. That's why I always like to be confident in His power and grace in my life and ministry. I love helping others solve their problems and encouraging them in their mourning's. I don't harbor negative feelings but rather build on the positive.

Quitting will never be an option for me, no matter what. I will not just sit back, sigh, and wish things would change. I will never allow life's circumstances to push me down and hold me under again. In my life and ministry, I have learned to take things easy. I believe that the overwhelming blessings of God will make me stronger in the Lord. Every year allows me to make successes in situations where I thought I had failed before.

I was flipping years a few days ago wondering just how resilient my family is. We are going to seize the future, shake off the self-limiting assumption that we are victims of circumstances, and resolve to live more graciously in Jesus Christ.

CHAPTER ELEVEN

TRANSFORMING THE YOUTH

YOUNG PEOPLE LOVE TO quote the promise, "I can do all things through Christ, who strengthens me" (Philippians 4:13). But that promise doesn't mean you can do whatever you want or what somebody else does. No. Paul is saying you can do anything God calls you to do, for with each of His assignment comes His assistance.

This verse actually teaches you to stay within the boundaries of what God called you to do, and do not try to undertake things that are not part of His will for you. That's not negativism; it is wisdom. God wants you to look to Him for your answers, not others. It just means that the plan that will lead you to success must come from God.

Find out now, before you start anything, what the will of God is for your life. Find it. Then, do it. Otherwise, you will live in frustration because of competing and trying to compare yourself with others. The Bible says, "A man must be content to receive the gift that is given to him from Heaven" (John 3:27). Learn to be content with anything that God gives you and move on. "You will do all things through He who strengthens me" (Philippians 4:13).

The church and the world are looking for young leaders. And for the last three years, we have been encouraging young people in the church to take up leadership positions. One of their greatest fears is the rate at which seemingly bright, talented, well-educated young leaders fall so spectacularly and often so abruptly. What every person should know is that succeeding in being a great leader is not through too many flaws but rather to rise above those flaws. There are a few nuggets that can help them prepare for leadership positions in the church and outside.

Having purpose and passion: when purpose and passion meet, there is nothing young people cannot accomplish as individuals, teams, or even organizations. A purpose-driven life makes leadership struggles come to an end. A lack of purpose make people not utilize their full potential, leading to frustration because deep inside lays the conviction that they can achieve more yet they are struck.

Tenacity in pursuit of leadership: No matter how tough the journey becomes; you should not give up. Everyday challenges youths encounter should give them an opportunity to question who they are.

Moral development: moral deficiencies lead to primitive development, rationalization, and blame game. All young people should take stock of their moral behavior, respect for social order, universal ethical principles, and conscience. For any leader to influence followers, he or she must have character infused with the highest level of moral development and admirable personality traits.

Ability to withstand pressure: to handle high-pressure and challenging tasks can be addictive. For some young leaders, with that level of pressure, in combination with opportunities to behave unethically, moments of truth will say a lot about their leadership. Being a good listener will help you to be a young leader. The best leaders are good listeners. Leaders dignify their followers by paying attention to their input and concerns. Young people should train to listen to others, especially those who give them good counsel.

Effective time management: young leaders should continuously discover what they are really doing with their time, checking on the day-to-day activities using an activity log to see what they really spend time on and if those activities are adding value or destroying value. This will help the youthful leaders to see whether their activities match up with their goals, desires, core values, and responsibilities. In the case of a mismatch, corrective action should be taken.

Embracing diversity: young leaders should be prepared to strategically blend new ways of thinking with the correct ways. They should note that being a leader is not an entitlement. It follows that they should have respect and creativity in helping the old generations understand why their new ways of thinking are making sense and learn how to earn buy-in. Paying attention to historical dynamics that exits even as they introduce new ideas is extremely important and can help minimize failures in leadership.

My own research shows that many young ladies are very qualified enough for top jobs. They are more qualified to start small businesses. But they don't want to start for many fake reasons, including family issues and other beliefs. My dear young lady, you can make it by just starting your own business. Ambition should be your key in anything you want to start. Just start. Ambition is what has very much brought powerful women to the top. It will get you, young lady, from where you are stuck now to the top. Don't shy again. Just be ambitious and start where you are and with what you have.

Ladies, there is nothing wrong with being self-confident and just starting. The time to start your small business is now. Just be focused and be intentional with your life. Put yourself before everyone else. Men succeed because they do that every time. They rely on their own money and ideas. This makes them strong enough to start any business. Take your time and be an ambitious lady.

Do you want a better life for yourself? Then, act now. Stop depending on others. Instead, depend on yourself. It's time to stop working for others' dreams and work for your own dream. Don't let anybody make you feel guilty for being yourself. Work hard with what you have, and God has promised to bless the work of your hands. Choose the business that suits you and just start. Don't let anybody stop you from pursuing your dreams. Don't let anybody intimidate you or make you feel less important because you are a woman. Tell everybody out there that you are wonderfully and fearfully made by God and that you deserve the best in life.

I encourage girls and young ladies to be strong and self-confident. They should be feeling sure about their own values and abilities. Many girls today lack the self-confidence needed to apply for senior jobs or start their own small businesses. I encouraged my daughter, Faith, to pursue a course in Business Information Technology [BIT]. This course involves mathematics and information technology in business. I tell her that every girl should depend on her ideas and work to be self-reliant so as to succeed in this life.

Faith is a successful girl who shows a lot of ambition in social situations, for she is able to understand how to stand strong during difficulties or complicated times in business. Faith and other business girls are more sophisticated these days. They are enduring the struggles that come with their business no matter what the situation may be.

In my life as a youth counselor, I have taught different girls who have grown to become very powerful women in society. I have seen young ladies become C.E.O.s and presidents in companies, as well as prime ministers, ministers, senators, and other important people in the world. Find your part in this world, young lady! There are many factors that contribute to greatness or success for such young ladies. The thing they have in life is ambition. This is what every girl or woman should have. As you start your business, thank God for bringing you this far.

Seriously consider this divine value: learn to practice temperance, which practically means practicing self-control. It means pausing and reflecting on all situations before acting. This virtue enables you to live a balanced life. Although I have narrated the bitter memories of my childhood, I could not have become a drug addict if I had known how to practice temperance as a young man. Today I am living a balanced life because I have learned to practice temperance. I want to help many young people to lead a better life.

To those who are married, they must seriously think about the meaning of their marriage vows before starting a business. You must pass the ultimate test of love and live by God's grace. In my life, I will thank God for giving me a chance to live after facing major challenges in my childhood. There is a lesson to be learned by others about my life; with my real-life experience, I know the importance of family. Without the support from a wife and children, I could not have helped others to overcome challenges. They helped me to display intelligence, boldness, composure, and leadership qualities that propel others to great heights.

I would like young people to excel and have a marriage that lasts. Learn to walk together. With your wife or husband, in all matters concerning money, identify one area that could pose the greatest danger to your marriage, because it is not spending money together. You need a lot of trust and transparence in business and all matters. Work with a budget that tells your money where it needs to go instead of wondering where it went.

Stay out of debt

DEBT IS THE WORST WAY to poverty. "The rich rule over the poor, and the borrower is a servant to the lender" (Proverbs 22:7). One of the worst things that can complicate and destroy our lives or marriages is financial debt. Through my own experience, I can warn that excessive debt makes life more complex and places great pressure on the borrower while also putting a tremendous burden on a marriage. Statistics say that this burden is so heavy that it's the root cause of much divorce today.

Our lifestyles make it very easy to get into debt. Glamorous advertisements can lure you into buying on credit. Credit card companies tell you that you don't have to pay right away. And banks attract you with their low interest rates and flexible payment methods. We also live in a time when people are impatient and want everything now with little care about the future.

Most people live in the moment, but the cold and hard truth is that tomorrow always comes when you are forced to deal with the results of what you did today. Many young people want to purchase things impulsively, hence incurring huge debts. Others buy more than they need; they seem to be addicted to staff and more staff things that do not add any real value to their lives.

While you should buy what you want by all means, you should not do so at the expense of going into debt. Learn to save money for things you want instead of buying them on credit. The word of God says, "He who gathers little by little will increase his riches" (Proverbs 13:11).

If you are already in debt, make a commitment to pay. Don't continue doing what you have done in the past because that will only make the problem worse. You may have to sacrifice for a while to pay your debt off. A debt hanging over your head is like an iron weight you are forced everywhere you go. Get rid of your debt and feel the freedom and simplicity that comes with owing nothing. The word of God encourages me, "Owe no one anything except to love one another, for he who loves another has fulfilled the law" (Romans 13:8). Live a balanced life by loving others.

CHAPTER TWELVE

MY CAMPAIGN AGAINST DRUG ABUSE AND HIV/AIDS

THIS OUTREACH PROJECT is sponsored by Stay Up Rehabilitative Community Based Organization and Gospel Messengers Church. This church is dedicated to knowing Christ and making Him known through evangelism and by meeting the needs of hurting people.

Vision:

Our vision is to: firstly, reach the unreached; secondly, give hope to the hopeless in this hurting world.

Administration:

Our organization, Stay Up Rehabilitative Community Based Organization was registered in the year 2020 to give hope to the hopeless. We are appealing to NGOs like world vision through KIABOGOKO to kindly support us in meeting people's health needs, especially prevention of HIV and AIDS, and other health problems.

We are working as a team of men and women in project management, development, and progress. We sometimes use evangelists, popular musicians, and actors to help the people to catch our vision. We use counselors to counsel the youth, widows, orphans, and the needy and hurting. We are monitoring, evaluating, and doing follow-up programming.

To achieve this vision of reaching the unreached, we are using handbills, posters, videos, and films on Christian values and moral values. During our outreach campaigns, evangelists and musicians help us to gather crowds. We've been making great impact during our outreach campaigns. During the day we do seminars, and during the night we show films and videos. Some young men and women do concerts or dramas. Films are very effective in winning souls and drawing crowds.

Project Objective:

To bring positive behavior change in sexual relationships and drug addictions.

Aim:

To reduce the risk of HIV/AIDS transmissions and drug addictions by providing

accurate information on:

Prevention:

We are promoting abstinence to teens and youths of the local community. We are using posters, charts, films, and books to warn the youth to avoid risky behaviors. We are extending our crusades throughout the local community. Targeted areas in the Elementaita Division include: Eburu, Baruku, Kiambogo Center, Elementaita Center, Kongasis Center, Camp Turkana, Tangitano, Oljorai, Tee, Morop, Munanda, Jogoo, Kanorero, and Njeru. Targeted groups of the project are youths, teens, and the local community. Some victims could require special treatments that we may not have; we refer them to government hospitals and other institutions.

Main Activities:

The project in our church mainly deals with crusades, workshops, seminars, and campaigns. We teach about HIV/AIDS and drug addictions as well as on how the victims can manage their lives by starting income-generating programs. We give them written materials. We ask the participants oral or written questions to help evaluation. We do follow-ups and monitor every workshop and seminar. We are targeting Nakuru Town, the Lanet Division, and the Bahati Division. In Nairobi we are targeting Githurai 45&44, Kasarani, Kibura, and Kawangware.

Facilitators:

We have counselors, teachers, doctors, and parents, as well as spiritual leaders like pastors. My team is responsible in organizing outreach programs. The facilitators must meet certain qualifications. They must teach on moral values. We do consider certain factors when selecting the right trainers. For those who cannot read or write, we talk and discuss. The common language we use in the outreach project is Kiswahili.

Approaches:

We are willing to work with the government, NGOs, churches, and ministries in making our project effective. We are reaching the needy, the hopeless, and the hurting out where they live, including in the villages, ghettos, and slums. The youth leaders help in collecting data of victims, widows, and orphans, as well as the number of victim deaths.

We use songs, dramas, poems, and books to teach participants. Sometimes we find that the materials that we will use will cost us a lot of money and wisdom in preparing them. To avoid these appointments during teaching sessions, we'd do a test of the materials before doing mass production.

We are the facilitators. Our staff writes a report after every session. We evaluate the performance of every facilitator. Every seminar, a workshop or session begins with prayers then an introduction of rules and the time to be taken by a session. Time varies from session to session.

Assessment:

We have assessment skills after every session. Sometimes we find out that some victims could require house visits, rehabilitation, counseling, or, with special cases, doctors. Sometimes our staff and youth leaders go around the division doing surveys on the behavioral changes of the youth and local communities.

The assessment surveys are very effective in the outreach project. The reports we come up with about the villagers are very encouraging after the seminars. We sometimes find that some facilitators did not change anybody in the villages; in which case, we could not invite him or her again. Before any session, we tell our facilitators not to pretend that they know everything but rather to let the teachings flow freely in the minds of the victims.

The truth will always set people free. We speak openly and give the listeners time to observe and learn a great deal from our sessions. We are also willing to learn from the listeners because they are human beings. This is how we know for sure whether they're truly learning something from our sessions.

Action:

Once we have analyzed the situation of the target groups or victims we are dealing with, we then specify what action we should take. From the assessment, we'd learn the victims' needs, attitudes, feelings, aspirations, and concerns, as well as their fears, which could hinder certain actions. Our emphasis is on positive behavior change. We teach participants where to get help as well as how to avoid HIV/AIDS transmission.

The project staff makes regular visits to the targeted areas and local communities to do assessments. The project is going a long way in helping the youth and the local communities. We are making follow-up visits to the victims in their homes and churches. The schoolteachers, pastors, and parents are giving us feedback from our seminars and workshops.

We are now planning to translate our books in Kiswahili to meet the needs of many victims living in East and Central Africa. Our materials and books are written to reflect on African cultures and problems that are affecting the local communities. We teach and cover topics on personal hygiene, safe and hazardous environments, sanitation, sex abuse, drug abuse, HIV/AIDS, peacekeeping, and income-generation programs.

Mission:

We are reaching the youth and the local communities by preaching the gospel of peace and love in this hurting world. We are targeting the youth because they are vulnerable to drug, alcohol, and sex abuse, as well as HIV/AIDS transmission. We have procedures, strategies, activities, and programs to reach the youth. We hold seminars, camps, conferences, and other available means of reaching teenagers before they perish in peer pressure or risky behaviors.

We sometimes use the media to reach the youth, even though it is very costly. Another effective strategy is publishing leaflets, tracts, newsletters, poster handbills, and books with touching messages and testimonies in them. Another very effective strategy is going house to house witnessing troubles and inviting people to the meetings, crusades, and campaigns.

We organize many teams of five young men and women and send them to certain villages, estates, ghettos, or slums; with the messages of salvation, healing, and deliverance. This strategy of witnessing house to house is very effective; the teams pray for the people and invite them into the venue of the big meeting.

We are using every available means to reach this crooked generation. We are willing to work with other churches and NGOs to make this vision a reality.

Financial Plan:

My office is working with a detailed budget for this outreach project. We are consulting with one accounting firm to help us in bookkeeping, financial planning, financial management, and banking details. We are looking for institutions and organizations that could be willing to work with us.

Recently, a meeting was held in the office headquarters of Nakuru to discuss a proposal based on project construction. We agreed to find some willing NGOs. The office found it necessary to adopt a policy of partnership with sponsors and donors.

We are planning to construct an outreach project office and rehabilitation centers for the victims of drug addiction in Nakuru County. In my speech as the presiding chairman who is the director of the outreach project, I stated that I'm trying to locate donors to help in the building of rehabilitation centers. We are praying and trusting in God to give us the right donors. I thanked pastors, teachers, and counselors who helped in teaching sessions.

Needs:

I've highlighted some of the needs that seemed to be emerging. A tent that could hold at least 2,000 people for seminars and workshops. Projectors to help in film-showing in the villages. A van and pickup to carry the staff and equipment into the venues.

I also suggested the start of a newsletter to report the outreach projects and developments. It would include features and pictures of victims, meetings, crusades, and campaigns. It would have brief testimonies of salvation, healing, and deliverances. It would include victims from all parts of Kenya and East and Central Africa.

The newsletter would give hope and encourage the youth in creativity and positive living or thinking.

It is encouraging to see victims saying "Yes" to Jesus and "No" to addiction, for Jesus are the answer in this hurting world.

Motto:

"I shall not die, but live and declare the works of the Lord" (Psalms 118:17). Together with you, I do believe that we are going to make great strides in rescuing the youth from perishing in drug addiction and sex abuse. That's why we are standing together as soldiers in the army of God. We are militant in our prayers, and we are joining hands with the government in the fight against the illicit brews and drug and sex abuse. We are tired of hearing about the untimely deaths of our youth from illicit brews and HIV/AIDS. We are helping the youth to say "No" to evil behaviors and say "Yes" to Jesus Christ.

I encourage the youth to follow a wide range of social interactions positively. I help them to identify a wide range of destructive emotions. I help them to connect with other youths in the world with positive behaviors and thinking.

Many youths are dying daily from the effects of the abuse of illicit drugs like cocaine, heroin, and the local illicit brews. The Church is helping the government in the campaigns to eradicate drug abuse and finish off all illicit brews in Kenya. The government has threatened to arrest all drug abusers and has sought to ban drug trafficking in Kenya.

Every day, the police, together with the administration, are doing patrols and holding war against drug abuse in Kenya. I have said that "I shall not die" because one day, during the time when I was high on drugs and the illicit brew called "chang'aa," the Lord saved and delivered me. I survived death by a whisker.

This is why I am rescuing the youth from perishing. Today, I am declaring that Jesus can set you free from drug abuse and sexual abuse. Having lived through so many trials, tragedies, and disappointments myself, I know well how to minister peace, hope, and love in these hurting souls. I have protected thousands of youths from perishing. I am a messenger of hope to drug addicts.

Troubled youth need somebody to listen to their plights. Somebody who can understand their feelings. The youth need a role model. I emulate Jesus Christ by preaching salvation, healing, and deliverance. I am helping sinners, drug addicts, prostitutes, orphans, widows, and the hopeless, needy, and hurting. I teach them how they can be saved, healed, and delivered from sins and diseases. Read my book, "I Shall Not Die," and you will never be the same again.

I am trying to help the youth overcome sexual lusts and drug addiction. I am transforming them from a crooked generation into a chosen generation. I am shaping their lives to help them become better mothers, fathers, and future leaders. I have written this book, Escape from Hell, which will help the youth to avoid all risky behaviors that could destroy their bodies and their lives.

I have changed thousands of the youth who are now helping in winning souls for Christ. Some of the former addicts are helping me to type the materials we are using in our outreach project. In my office, I receive many testimonies from those who have been saved, healed, changed, transformed, or delivered. I also receive letters of encouragement and calls from the youth who have become helped or blessed by this project.

I have a big vision and a big project for the youth. I like to crack jokes and interact with the youth. I am imbued with a love, desire, and determination to reach the youth to progress and show them how to overcome setbacks, failures, barriers, obstacles, and hindrances so that they can succeed in their work.

It is my greatest joy to see a young person blossoming until the great day of marriage. I am encouraging the youth to obey their parents and teachers and be role models to children. I advise them to work with their spiritual leaders. Not only do I prove to be a blessing to the young generation, but they are also a blessing to me as well. They bless me in their worshipping, praising, and testimonies.

Sometimes in the youth camps, youth conventions, and youth seminars, I lack the words to express my amount of joy and appreciation to the youths. I am very glad to be playing a very important part in building and strengthening the faith of these future leaders. My vision, my burden, is to reach this crooked generation. I'm ready to go into schools, colleges, streets, and homes to rescue the youth before they perish.

I invite you to be part of this great vision. I'm always preparing materials or tools to help me reach and shape the destiny of these future husbands and wives. I teach them and also allow them to teach others (2 Timothy 2:2). I am tirelessly working in creating awareness through sensitization and seminars for the youth, particularly on HIV/AIDS prevention.

We are reflecting on activities that are geared toward improving their lives through behavior change. Through my experience, I have come to realize that leadership development and behavior change in the youth is a process we cannot teach the youth in a short time. It is a long process. I encourage the youth not to rely on a job for that process because God doesn't look at the kind of work you are doing or the location you are in. God blesses you no matter what you are doing or where you are.

As an example, Jacob and David were mere shepherds, but Jacob became a very rich man while David was promoted from a shepherd to a king. Joseph was promoted from a house boy to the prime minister of Egypt.

Considering the present global financial crisis of the whole world, you need not to choose which job you can do. Do any job you find. God promises to bless any work of your hands. The Bible encourages, "Whatever your hands find to do, do it with all you might, for there is no work or thought or knowledge or wisdom in the grave where you are going" (Ecclesiastes 9:10).

Africa is dangling its feet precariously over the edge of global financial meltdown. This is one of the signs of the end times. We are living in the competitive times. The ongoing world recession has certainly had an adverse effect on our economic problems and an inevitable impact on our lives and jobs. That's why millions of people, including the youth, are suffering. Let me say that Africa's future is entirely in the hands of the youth. A lack of future visions, dreams, and goals is bringing short-sightedness to our youth. We are in need of a progressive change in our youth and in our nations.

I'm preparing the youth to be responsible leaders. Africa must lift up her head from the sand and begin to tackle her economic problems so that her people can enjoy their lives. The youth have a leading role to play in reversing these ominous situations. I'm encouraging the youth on how to be leaders in their lives and how they can overcome the present economic crises. I'm teaching the youth how they can live with each other in peace, for without peace, nobody will see God. I tell them that justice in any society cannot be restored by the use of violence, since it is not justified. I am an ambassador of peace to the youth. Jesus, the Prince of Peace, is my Redeemer; my Redeemer lives.

I'm part of the process of leadership development in the youth. I am a mentor for the youth and teens. My ministry has one big youth conference a year in the month of December. I have many years invested into the ministry in shaping the lives of the youth. Please pray or give me support for this outreach project to the youth.

I always feel very humbled and honored whenever I'm invited to teach the youth and minister to them. With my help and my ministry's help, many young people have been rescued, saved, transformed, healed, and delivered.

My prayers are that God will continue to help me in reaching and ministering to the youth and that more people will plan to be part of this wonderful outreach project. God bless you as you echo the cry together with us: "Africa for Jesus!" My vision is reaching the unreached in Africa.

CHAPTER THIRTEEN

LIVE RIGHT

I REMEMBER HOW IT ALL began. It was 1978, just some minutes after drinking the illicit brew known as "chang'aa." My life was a mess, and I grew tired of living any longer in this world of evil and sins. Evil thoughts of committing suicide flashed in my mind. I was alone in my small hut. This was one of the darkest and loneliest times of my life. Everything seemed to be so confusing as many questions about life were boiling inside of me. "It'd be better for me to try life in the next world!" I thought, alone.

I had no money. I had no good clothes. I had no good house. I had no job that had prestige. I was very anxious to know what my life was all about. I questioned myself, and all of these questions were demanding answers before I ended my life once and for all. I came to experience the evil things that youngest people experience after abusing drugs. The world could not give me the answers that I needed so urgently.

But on the table of my hut, I found an old Bible that my brother, David, had given me to read; I hadn't had time to read it. For the first time, I opened the Bible and read the Word: "I came so that they might have life and might have it abundantly" (John 10:10). I thanked God that in the Bible I found the answer to my life that I had been seeking for all those years. I found hope in the word of God. Hope is the essence of life. I read again the Word about eternal life; abundant life. These words were ringing in my soul. This was a direct answer to the many questions I was asking myself.

I realized that God had a purpose for my life. I understood that God created me so that I might enjoy life and, secondly, that I might serve Him in this hurting world. Now I urgently needed a new life, for the Bible showed me that I was a sinner who had fallen short of the glory of God. In Christ, there was a solution for my problem, but little did I know that Jesus loves me. The key is that I believe in God's son, Jesus Christ, as my personal Savior. I decided to confess my sins and accept Him as my personal Savior. Suddenly, as I cried to Jesus, He entered into my heart. I was totally changed, saved, and transformed. I was a new creation.

In Christ, I crossed from death to eternal life. Before my salvation, I thought of committing suicide, which would lead me to perish in hell. Now I hated death; although, hate isn't a Christian virtue. But if there was ever anything that was easy to hate in my life, it was death. No matter how carefully we prepare, death comes suddenly at an unexpected time. And it always leaves behind a legacy of sorrow and loneliness. Death takes infants, adults, sinners, saints, kings, and the poor. But in Jesus Christ, I had hope because the Bible says, "For as in Adam, all die; but even so in Christ, all shall be made alive" (1 Corinthians 15:22). I was made alive in Christ; I crossed over from death to eternal life. Hating death, or dreading it, doesn't do any good.

The only effective way to deal with death is to accept Jesus Christ as your personal Savior. In Him, death is swallowed up in victory. Paul asked, "O' death, where is your sting? O' grave, where is your victory?" Thanks be to God, for He has given us victory over death through Jesus Christ. Read I Corinthians 15:54–57. God will accomplish His purposes in my life, even though He may use unusual means: "For you died and your life is now hidden with Christ in God" (Colossians 3:3).

"God, who at sundry times and in diverse manners, spoke in time past unto us by prophets; hath in these days spoken unto us by His Son" (Hebrews 1:1–2). When I first heard the voice of God echoing in my soul, I understood that God is real, but how could I go back to Him? The words stood: "Except ye repent, ye shall all perish" (Luke 13:3). This is God's own judgment, and I had no appeal.

If you want to go on a long safari, say about one million miles, you will begin with a step. And the first step in this everlasting safari is by absolute repentance of every sin in your life. Next, you forsake sins and then receive Jesus Christ in your soul by faith. No one can be saved unless he or she repents and is therefore born again by the power of God. Jesus came to seek and save those of whom were lost, and I was one of them. He came so that we might have life. "In Him was life, and the life was the light of men" (John 1:4).

Be Born Again

We must forsake our natural life in order to be given eternal life. That is why Jesus told Nicodemus, a morally upright religious leader, "Except a man is born again, he cannot see the Kingdom of God" (John 3:3). Our first birth made us children of wrath because of the sinful nature we inherited from our fore-father, Adam. The second birth makes us partakers of the nature of God.

When I repented of my sins, Jesus was formed inside me. He lives in me and watches over my life. The instant you take Him as your Savior, salvation will be an accomplished fact. The Bible states, "He came unto His own, and His own received Him not. But to the many who received Him, to them He gave the power to become the sons of God" (John 1:11–12).

When I repented and received Jesus Christ as my personal Savior, He came and exchanged His life with mine. My sins went out by repentance, and He came into my heart by rejuvenation. "The Lord is ... not willing that any should perish, but all should come to repentance" (2 Peter 3:9). "He is able also to save them who come unto God by Him" (Hebrews 7:25). "In Him, we have redemption through His blood, and the forgiveness of sins, according to the riches of His grace" (Ephesians 1:7). What a wonderful Savior Jesus is!

. . . .

DON'T PERISH

Before Jesus came into my life, God had justly condemned me to hell, for I was never righteous; not even once. But through His great love, which He showed to my life, He offered me the wonderful gift of salvation. I know that in the sight of God, whether spiritual or natural, sin is a serious detriment between man and God. Jesus crashed the barriers and became life to mankind. Peter said, "Being born again—not of corruptible seed, but of incorruptible—by the word of God" (1 Peter 1:23). Jesus said, "That which is born of the Flesh is flesh, and that which is born of the Spirit is spirit" (John 3:6). Are you born again by the power of God? Please, repent now; otherwise, you will perish in hell.

Salvation, Not Religion

The most awful and regrettable aspect of those who are lost in religious sects are not that they worship the devil but that they have refused to repent of their sins. Despite that their leaders keep on soothing their consciences Sunday after Sunday, telling them, "We shall all go to heaven, just as we are." The witness of God testified of his son, Jesus. And he who believeth shall not be damned. God's first commandment (Exodus 20:1–3) leaves no doubt about who should be worshipped. And until one is born again and able to worship God in truth and in spirit, there shall always remain an empty void in his or her soul. Take note that any religion without settled peace for the conscience is the devil's counterfeit.

Don't Be a Hypocrite

Let us digress for a moment and consider the outward shows of Christianity under the name of religious services. The pretending minister evidently knows nothing of the Scripture in relation to repentance. His only thought is to make a good show of his religion. The beautifully clad minister is the showstopper before the congregation, and you can see him moving towards the pulpit with solemn airs and dignified, calculated steps, followed by other little stars stylishly dressed in colorful uniforms.

They sing before the congregation with a sweet voice, making the choir angelic in outward appearance, and yet not even one of them is born again. They prefer to hurt the truth of God against all shame and hypocrisy, for it hits harder and echoes louder to present lies.

Listen to the sermons of these so-called sect leaders. Never will they speak a word of repentance of sin. The judgment day for sinners and the lake of fire await unbelievers. Never a word spoken on the coming of our Lord, Jesus Christ, here on Earth again. Instead, they are smooth talkers, men pleasers, blind leaders, and pretentious ministers of our age.

I always ask myself: Can a born-again believer with in-dwelling power of Christ's life sit back silently under such awful spiritless ministries of blind leaders? Oh, no! Can I leave all these millions of souls in the wrong hands to perish in hell by refusing to use the spiritual gift God has given me so as to not offend such leaders? No! I would rather die pleading with people to repent.

Repent or Otherwise Perish

Many people are still trapped within the bondage of sin in their religious sects. The sects are what they profess to be life, more so than the Savior, Jesus Christ. "He who covereth his sins shall not prosper" (Proverbs 28:13). "God now commanded all men everywhere to repent" (Acts 17:30). "Except ye repent, ye shall likewise perish" (Luke 13:3). Will you die in your sins because of your unbelief? Shake off the spirit of religion and embrace true salvation by genuine repentance. Declare that—I shall not die.

About Us

Gospel Messengers Church is a nonprofit dedicated to transforming lives in Kenya's most marginalized communities. Committed to eradicating female genital mutilation (FGM), poverty, and illiteracy, the organization builds schools, provides clean water through boreholes, and empowers communities through education and sustainable development.

By addressing social injustices and uplifting vulnerable populations, Gospel Messengers Church fosters hope and opportunity for the less fortunate.

You can Donate via M-Pesa Pay Bill no: 880100 a/c: 5146870014.

You can also use PayPal email: messengergospel13@gmail.com

THESE ARE OUR BANK DETAILS FOR INTERNATIONAL MONEY TRANSFERS.

Bank Name	NCBA BANK KENYA PLC
Branch Name	NAKURU
Branch Code	000 (for any branch)
Bank Full Address	P.O. BOX 44599–00100, NAIROBI – KENYA
Bank Account Name	GOSPEL MESSENGER CHURCH
Bank Code	07
Bank Account Number	5146870014
SWIFT /BIC Code	CBAFKENX

Also by Peter N Muya

Kill Me Not
Love Without Lust
Do Not Weep
Death From Illicit Brew
Hope For Survival
I Shall Not Die
Never Lose Hope

Watch for more at https://www.gospelmessengerschurch.com.

www.ingramcontent.com/pod-product-compliance
Lightning Source LLC
Chambersburg PA
CBHW071440130726

47997CB00006B/2164